Presented to

Chuck Drum

By

On the Occasion of

Birthday

Date

September 17, 1999

*from Frank
Lou
Dove*

A HEART LIKE HIS

DISCOVERING THE HEART OF JESUS IN THE FRUIT OF THE SPIRIT

Mike & Amy Nappa

BARBOUR
PUBLISHING, INC.
Uhrichsville, Ohio

A HEART
LIKE HIS

A Heart Like His is another creative resource from the authors
at Nappaland Communications, Inc. To contact the authors
send e-mail to: *Nappaland@aol.com*

Published by Barbour Publishing, Inc., P.O. Box 719,
Uhrichsville, OH 44683 http://www.barbourbooks.com

Member of the
Evangelical Christian
Publishers Association

This book is lovingly dedicated to the memory of Wilfred Townsend, a man who exhibited a heart like Christ's in our every encounter with him.

Though he passed away more than two years ago, we are thankful for Grand Wil's example and still remember him with great fondness, anticipating the day when we will be joyfully reunited with him in heaven.

CONTENTS

Against such things there is no law!

INTRODUCTION:
PAUL'S LITTLE GROCERY LIST

He rattles them off quickly, as if he's simply listing the first things that come to his mind. "The fruit of the Spirit," Paul says in the book of Galatians, "is love, joy, peace, patience, kindness, goodness, faithfulness, gentleness and self-control" (5:22–23 NIV).

Then, almost as an afterthought, he adds, "Against such things there is no law."

I read those words today and wonder: Did Paul realize he was writing a letter that would someday be called the Word of God? Did he know the difference his little grocery list of character qualities would make in the lives of millions of people? In the lives of people like me and you?

Honestly, I don't know. But I do know the words Paul spoke in Galatians 5:22–23 carry with them a challenge—and an invitation. A challenge to become the kind of person whose life is characterized by these qualities; an invitation to allow God's Spirit to work in our hearts and make the fulfillment of that challenge possible.

Which brings us to this book. Not long ago,

my wife, Amy, and I sat down and began asking ourselves, "What does the fruit of the Spirit really mean? How does it bring about in us a heart like Christ's?" This book is the result of our searching thus far. Of course it doesn't contain all the answers, but we hope it has a few. Of course it doesn't ask all the questions either, but we hope it inspires a few new ones.

So are you ready to join us in our exploration of Paul's little grocery list? Then turn the page and let's get on our way. Our prayer is that reading this book will bless you as much as the writing of it has blessed us.

—Mike Nappa, Winter 1999

1

The Fruit of the Spirit Is...

LOVE

Imagine, if you will, a world without love of any kind. It's a bleak, desolate world, isn't it? Where there is no love, there is no joy, no satisfaction, no comfort, no home.

But that's not the kind of world God has created—or intended—for us. And so it's no surprise that the first quality listed among the fruit of the Spirit is love, for, as 1 John 4:16 tells us, "God is love."

A HERO'S LOVE

I keep his picture in my office, in a place where I'll see it every day. It's a picture of Bill Gale. I don't know what he does for a living, or even if he's a Christian. All I really know about him is that he volunteers at a local hospital in the New York City area. Seven years ago I saw his picture in a magazine and he's been my hero ever since.

Let me describe him for you. He's an average-looking man, mid-fifties probably. Narrow shoulders. A hint of pudginess around his middle. Thinnish face. Bald—but denying it by combing a few wispy strands of hair from one side of his head to the other. By all appearances, not really the hero type. But it's what he's doing in that picture that inspires me.

He's holding a baby.

That's it. Nothing more. Just holding a baby. You see, thanks to the mother's drug habit, this infant was born with an addiction to crack cocaine. Doctors say they can't do much for the child—it must break the habit cold turkey.

Where doctors fail, Bill steps in. He can't perform surgery. He can't oversee a blood transfusion. He can't even fill out the hospital forms in triplicate. But he can give a little love to one so helpless it hurts.

Bill cuddles infants. He whispers sweet nothings to them, rocks them, warms them, smiles at them, holds and heals them. They'll never remember Bill, or even know he was there, but he keeps doing it anyway. And because some photographer caught him in the act, I have a picture of what unconditional love looks like.

Every time I gaze at that picture, I see more than just Bill and a baby. I see me—a sin-addicted infant—helpless, in pain, crying for someone to love me. And I see my heavenly Father reaching out to hold me. And I realize Bill Gale is only a dim reflection of the unconditional love that brought Jesus to this earth in the first place, and that made Him willing to die in my place.

That's why Bill Gale is my hero. He reminds me of our eternal Hero's love.

Lavished on me.

10 REASONS TO SAY "I LOVE YOU" TO OTHERS

1. Because God said it to you first.

2. Because if you say it enough, people might actually believe it.
3. Because if you don't, they might forget.
4. Because today may be the last time you see them.
5. Because it's a unique opportunity to make someone feel special.
6. Because it makes a heart smile.
7. Because it could prompt someone to say the same to you.
8. Because it's free, but still manages to pays great dividends.
9. Because love is spoken in any language.
10. Because, well. . .because you love them!

❧

10 CREATIVE WAYS TO SAY "I LOVE YOU" TO OTHERS

1. Spell it in soap on the bathroom mirror.
2. Sing it into a tape recorder and mail it to someone you love.
3. Write it on the back of a jigsaw puzzle, then give the puzzle to a loved one, saying there's a "secret message" on the back.

4. Write it on a yellow sticky note, then attach the note to your forehead and kiss your spouse so he or she can read it up close.
5. Cut out the words in the shape of a bookmark, and put it in your son or daughter's schoolbook.
6. Write it in sunblock on your shoulder, then lie out until the words show up like a tattoo. Show your sunblock tattoo to loved ones.
7. Hug.
8. Pray.
9. Send a valentine in any month except February. (Might as well send some of those candy hearts too!)
10. Share your chocolate. (Need we say more?)

❧

10 WEAK EXCUSES PEOPLE GIVE FOR NOT SAYING "I LOVE YOU" TO OTHERS

1. They already know.
2. I told them once, and I haven't changed my mind yet.

3. I don't like to share my feelings much.
4. They might not love me back.
5. I don't want to embarrass anyone—myself included.
6. Men don't do those kinds of things.
7. I forgot.
8. They should be able to tell by my actions.
9. I'm angry at that person.
10. They never shared chocolate with me.

ॐ

Sometimes we substitute our devotion to sinful habits as expressions of love. And, like the man in this story by John Duckworth, we suffer the consequences. . .

THE MAN WHO LOVED PORCUPINES

You know the doctor down on Seventh Street? The so-called heart specialist? Yeah, that's the one. If you ever have a problem don't go to see him. The guy's a quack. I mean I went to him with this problem, but he couldn't fix it. Cost me twenty-five bucks to see him, and all he did was throw up his hands as if there were nothing he could do!

It went like this. I sat down on the examination table, and he asked, "So, what seems to be the problem?"

I explained, "Well, doc, I don't know exactly. I keep having these pains in my chest. Shooting pains. Maybe it's my heart."

"Hmm," he muttered. "Take off your shirt, and I'll have a listen."

So I took off my shirt. As soon as I did, this guy just about had a heart attack himself. "Hey!" he said. "What are all those puncture wounds on your chest?"

"Oh, they're nothin'," I breezed.

"Nothing?" he protested. "Son, those are serious wounds. There must be two dozen of them."

"Not counting the ones in my arms," I added.

He looked at my arms and whistled. Then he frowned. "All right," he said. "What happened?"

"Nothin', really. Just a porcupine, that's all."

"A porcupine?" he cried. "Son, to get this many wounds, you'd have to pick up a porcupine with your bare hands and hug it."

"Right," I said. "That's what I did."

He looked at me with a really weird expression. "You hugged a porcupine?" he questioned. "Why would you want to do a thing like that?"

I shrugged. "I'm just into that, I guess. I like porcupines."

He took off his glasses and looked down his nose at me—just like my old man always does. "Son," he said, "you just can't do that. Porcupines aren't good for you. They're dangerous. They can stick you full of quills."

"So?" I said. "Don't knock it until you've tried it."

He shook his head. "I don't have to try it to know it's not good for me. Now promise me you'll stay away from porcupines."

"Hey," I said. "Are you a heart specialist or not? I've got chest pains. What are you going to do about it?"

That's when he threw up his hands. "There's nothing I can do, unless you give up hugging porcupines," he said. Then he put a bandage on my chest and sent me out the door.

Can you believe that guy? I mean, talk about self-righteous! Where does he get off judging my lifestyle? If I want to hug porcupines, that's my business. His job is to get rid of chest pains!

Anyway, I left and went over to the zoo. Sure enough, there were some great porcupines there. I sneaked into the cage, picked one up, and for some reason those chest pains started again. I mean, I thought I was gonna die.

So that's why I'm here, doc. You're a heart specialist, too, right? You've gotta help me. Maybe I need open heart surgery or a transplant or something, huh?

What? You want me to see the guy next door? What kind of doctor is he?

Well, why won't you tell me? What's—

Hey, who are these guys coming through the door? Where are you taking me? I don't want to put on that jacket—

You people are all alike! Trying to crush my alternative lifestyle, imposing your worn-out morality! I'll get you for this! I'll—I'll—

Wait!

I'll. . .uh. . .make you a deal.

No more heart specialists.

How about lots of. . .acupuncture?

SPEAKING OF LOVE. . .

"Love alters not with his brief hours and weeks, but bears it out even to the edge of doom."

—WILLIAM SHAKESPEARE, in *Sonnet 116*

"There are moments, most unexpectedly, when something inside me tries to assure me that. . . love is not the whole of a man's life. . . .Then comes a sudden jab of red-hot memory and all this 'commonsense' vanishes like an ant in the mouth of a furnace."

—C. S. LEWIS, while mourning the death of his wife in *A Grief Observed*

*"Love is foolish. . .
but I still might try it sometime."*

JILL, age 6,
in an Internet posting

"Love doesn't just sit there, like a stone, it has to be made, like bread; re-made all the time, made new."

—URSULA K. LE GUIN,
in *The Lathe of Heaven*

"Don't do things like have smelly, green sneakers. You might get attention, but attention ain't the same thing as love."

—ALONZO, age 9,
in another Internet posting

"People who are empty inside and hungry for the love that was denied them in childhood will often risk anything—even the suffering, degradation and death of AIDS—in order to grab just a little fleeting affection."

—KEVIN GRAHAM FORD and JIM DENNEY,
in *Jesus for a New Generation*

*"Hatred paralyzes life; love releases it.
Hatred confuses life; love harmonizes it.
Hatred darkens life; love illumines it."*

MARTIN LUTHER KING JR.,
in *Strength to Love*

"Many who have spent a lifetime in it can tell us less of love than the child that lost a dog yesterday."

—THORNTON WILDER, as quoted in
The American Scholar Reader

"This is true love—a love that continues when we don't feel like it; a love that's unconditional; a love that rejoices in good times and encourages in bad times; a love that lasts forever. That willful, decisive love is what Jesus has for [us]."

—MIKE NAPPA, AMY NAPPA,
and MICHAEL WARDEN, in *Get Real*

છ૪

Occasionally—no, often—love is a risky business. Mother Teresa proved that time and again, even if it meant risking all to save people some thought were not worth saving. . .

IMPOSSIBLE POSSIBILITIES OF LOVE

"Impossible," they said. "You'll be killed!"

But Mother Teresa refused to believe them, and refused to back down.

It was during a time of seemingly endless military conflict in Lebanon. Heavy bombing had trapped thirty-seven "special needs" children in a hospital deep inside the war-torn city of Beirut, Lebanon.

"They are as good as dead," said some.

"Let them die," said others.

Because the fighting still continued, no one was willing to risk an attempt to rescue the children. No one, that is, except Mother Teresa. When she heard of the plight of the thirty-seven, she didn't hesitate.

A frail-looking old woman, Mother Teresa stood only four-feet, eleven-inches tall and weighed less than 100 pounds. But she was a small woman with great love, and she would not sit idly by while these children became just another story of the devastation of war. She determined to let nothing stop her from saving those little ones—not bombs, not guns, and certainly not people telling her it was too risky.

Mother Teresa quickly flew to Beirut and immediately began making arrangements for the rescue. She informed everyone that she would go into the city the next day, "When the fighting stops." It was then she planned to bring out the children.

People looked at her in disbelief, possibly muttering "crazy" under their breath. Love or no love, they knew there'd be no break in the fighting—it had been going on for months! And it seemed that they were right. The fighting continued.

Through the night. Into the morning, bullets and bombs raged until. . .

At precisely the time Mother Teresa had indicated, peace fell over the city. Guns were silent; bombs were held at bay. Unshaken despite the opposition to her cause, Mother Teresa boarded an ambulance, drove deep into the war zone, and brought all thirty-seven children out of danger and into safety. Only after her work was finished did the fighting resume.

Mother Teresa once said, "We can do no great things, only small things with great love." She proved that with her life and her willingness to risk life for the sake of love.

❧

THE WORD ON LOVE

"Love is patient, love is kind. It does not envy, it does not boast, it is not proud. It is not rude, it is not self-seeking, it is not easily angered, it keeps no record of wrongs. Love does not delight in evil but rejoices with the truth. It always protects, always trusts, always hopes, always perseveres. Love never fails."

—1 Corinthians 13:4–8

"This is love: not that we loved God, but that he loved us and sent his Son as an atoning sacrifice for our sins. Dear friends, since God so loved us, we also ought to love one another. No one has ever seen God; but if we love each other, God lives in us and his love is made complete in us."

—1 John 4:10–12

"But God demonstrates his own love for us in this: While we were still sinners, Christ died for us."

Romans 5:8

"The Lord appeared to us in the past, saying: 'I have loved you with an everlasting love; I have drawn you with loving-kindness.' "

—Jeremiah 31:3

"[Jesus said] 'A new command I give you: Love one another. As I have loved you, so you must love one another. All men will know that you are my disciples if you love one another."

—John 13:34–35

UNTITLED POEM BY
MICHELANGELO (1475–1564)[1]

If it be true that any beauteous thing
    Raises the pure and just desire of man
From earth to God, the eternal fount of all,
    Such I believe my love; for as in her
So fair, in whom I all besides forget
    I view the gentle work of her Creator,
I have no care for any other thing
    Whilst thus I love. Nor is it marvelous,
Since the effect is not of my own power,
    If the soul doth by nature, tempted forth,
Enamored through the eyes,
    Repose upon the eyes, which it resembleth,
And through them riseth to the primal love,
    As to its end, and honors in admiring;
For who adores the Maker must love his
    work.

LOVE SPEAKS TRUE[2]

Ed Rowell, editor for *Leadership* magazine, relates this humorous story about love:

A husband asked his wife, "Tell me, Dear, have you ever been in love before?"

She thought a moment and replied, "No, Darling. I once respected a man for his great intelligence. I admired another for his remarkable courage. I was captivated by yet another for his good looks and charm. But with you, well, how else could you explain it except love?"

❧

IT'S ALL GREEK TO ME

During the time when the New Testament was written, the Greek language employed many words to describe the different aspects of love. The three most commonly used words, however, were these:

- *Eros*
- *Philia*
- *Agape*

In his excellent resource, the *Expository Dictionary of Bible Words,* theologian Lawrence O. Richards tells more about those Greek terms.

Eros embodied the love a man has for a woman and a woman has for a man, explains Richards. That includes sexual desires and physical intimacy. Richards notes that, surprisingly, "This word, much used in Greek culture, is not found in the New Testament."

Philia, Richards reveals, was the most common word for love. Though no religious meaning was attached to it in Greek culture, it indicated a "fondness which develops as persons are attracted to each other and build a relationship within or outside the context of family. Loving behavior, which is appropriate between relatives or friends."

Agape, (pronounced "Uh-GOP-Ay"), Richards says, "was chosen by the New Testament writers to convey to future generations the unique dimensions and overwhelming depth of God's love and to explore the impact of that love on human beings."

Now, thinking back on your life experience,

which Greek word most describes your experience with love? Which do you most desire to experience? What can you do about that today?

☙

BEDTIME

Last night I went to tuck my son into bed.

I gently arranged the covers, pushed a stray hair out from his eyes,

Leaned close to kiss his cheek and whispered, "I love you."

Instead of saying the same back to me,

He simply smiled and said, "I know."

I paused. How did he know that? I asked.

Rolling his eyes as if I'd asked the dumbest question on earth,

He quickly responded,

"Dad, you tell me that every day. That's how I know."

After a quick hug, I went into the living room.

My wife was reading there.

For no particular reason, I said to her, "I love you."

She simply smiled and said, "I know."

2

The Fruit of the Spirit Is. . .

JOY

After years of deep theological study, Bible school degrees, and eons of church attendance, we finally discovered only a few years back something that changed our lives dramatically: God is a joyful Person!

What a difference it makes to know that God is smiling, not frowning, on His children; to know He's preparing a place for us in heaven where we can bask in His joyful presence for all eternity; and to know He has placed a little bit of His joy in our lives today. The real question, then, is: What are we going to do with that joy?

Recipe for a Joyful Day

Ingredients:
- One relationship with God
- ½ cup gratefulness
- A sprinkling of songs in your heart
- A heaping spoonful of prayer
- A tablespoon of children's giggles
- A dollop of humor
- A dash of sunshine (optional)
- One pair rose-colored glasses (optional)

Lay out one relationship with God as the base. Add gratefulness, songs, and prayer. Mix thoroughly. Next, fold in giggles, humor, and sunshine. Bake overnight with a good night's sleep. Serve with cheerful attitude and joyful determination. Feeds the hungry hearts of one to millions.

EMPEROR NORTON

Some called him crazy. Others called him a fool. But most San Franciscans in the late 1800s called him Emperor.

Emperor Norton, that is.

His official title was "Emperor of the United States and Protector of Mexico." He "ruled" San Francisco from 1857 to 1880, spreading smiles and joviality. He was just a man with a happy attitude, a merchant who had tried to corner the rice market—and lost his fortune. Yet, after going from riches to poverty, Norton refused to accept that he had to lose his joy. He "crowned" himself and began parading around the streets of San Francisco in full costume as emperor.

There was something so appealing about a man who insisted on enjoying life that the people of the City by the Bay went along with the charade. The good king was granted front row seats at every theater opening. Tailors carefully created and mended his regal plumed hat, cane, and uniform at no cost. The finest restaurants served this monarch their best meals free. The railroads offered transportation "so he could address his subjects." Emperor Norton even had an honorary seat in the state legislature!

How did a man with few financial means earn such a lavish lifestyle? He dealt in a currency that's all too rare—the currency of smiles. His "Majesty" always brought a smile to the faces of others; like the time he ordered a bridge be built to span the bay—the Golden Gate Bridge; or when he decreed that a giant Christmas tree be raised in Union Square for the children of his kingdom.

We can learn a lot from this would-be sovereign. If we would win the hearts of our children, we must be willing to share with them a simple, lasting joy that Jesus gives to life. When we do, our children, like the people of San Francisco, will remember us with fondness.

Funny thing about Emperor Norton. You, too, have probably gotten a little joy from this so-called crazy man. Mark Twain immortalized the emperor in the character of his pauper "king" in the classic novel *The Adventures of Huckleberry Finn*. If you've read the book, you, too, have met the "emperor" of the United States and "protector" of Mexico.

THE WORD ON JOY

"So I commend the enjoyment of life, because nothing is better for a man under the sun than to eat and drink and be glad."

—Ecclesiastes 8:15

"A happy heart makes the face cheerful, but heartache crushes the spirit. . . . A cheerful heart is good medicine."

—Proverbs 15:13, 17:22

"As the Father has loved me, so have I loved you. Now remain in my love. If you obey my commands, you will remain in my love, just as I have obeyed my Father's commands and remain in his love. I have told you this so that my joy may be in you and that your joy may be complete."

—John 15:9–11

"The LORD has done great things for us, and we are filled with joy."

—Psalm 126:3

"This is the day the LORD has made; let us rejoice and be glad in it."

—Psalm 118:24

"The joy of the LORD is your strength."

—Nehemiah 8:10

"Be joyful always."

—1 Thessalonians 5:16

❧

In his delightfully eloquent book, Dangerous Wonder, *Michael Yaconelli shares about a time of pure, unadulterated, youthful joy. We enjoyed Michael's joyful reminiscing so much, we had to share it with you here. . .*

WILD ABANDON

It was the '50s—1952 to be exact. At ten years old, my everyday agenda had one focus—playing. Each day would bring a new challenge as my friends and I determined what activity would capture our attention. We lived in a lower economic neighborhood populated with hundreds of children who never felt poor, never thought about what we didn't have, what we were "deprived" of. We only knew that the options for playing were endless—marbles, street stickball tournaments, Ping-Pong championships, hide-and-seek, squirt-gun fights, swimming at the city pool, riding our bikes to the sugar beet factory, exploring boxcars at isolated train tracks. There were no televisions to distract us (most of our families couldn't afford one), no video games to swallow up the time. All we had was our imaginations.

Looking back at those years, I realize our imaginations were more than enough to keep us busy and make us wish the days were longer. Oh, there were some hot July days in southern California when our energy was sapped and we would complain about "nothing to do." Our parents were not very sympathetic. "There is plenty to do!" they would point out. "And if you can't find anything to do, we have some chores you can do." It didn't take long for us to occupy ourselves.

One July morning as my friends and I were sitting around on our bikes, daydreaming about what might be that day's adventure, Jimmy blurted out, "Let's build a spaceship!" The moment the words left his mouth, we knew destiny had spoken. Three boys on Evergreen Street were to build a spaceship. No one said a word, yet it was clear what we were to do. Our assignments were obvious; we knew instinctively who would do what. Jimmy, the ham operator's son, would be the communications officer and in charge of the radio and engineering components. I was in charge of the spaceship structure—my dad worked at Sears, a great source for rocket shells, otherwise known as refrigerator boxes. Alan was in charge of logistics—his dad was in construction and Alan was very strong. He was also the navigator.

The construction of the spaceship took three full days. My backyard was chosen as the launchpad and subsequent space location, much to my parents' chagrin. It took two days to haul the exterior of the spaceship into place, another day to construct its interior, and then one full day to familiarize ourselves with our new surroundings so that everyone knew his role and was comfortable with his section of the spaceship, and to ensure that all the commands and destinations were mapped out and understood.

We were the envy of the neighborhood, with space voyages occurring daily for weeks. I don't remember how many weeks because, while our spaceship was "operational," we were oblivious to time. Every morning we could hardly wait to get done with our chores and get back in the spaceship. The time went by quickly. For most of the summer our world was our spaceship, where we miraculously survived meteor attacks, intergalactic battles with alien enemies, internal explosions, attempted mutinies, and mysterious forces of evil. There were many other crises we managed to overcome—Jimmy was grounded for a week when it was discovered he had equipped his communications center with his dad's most expensive equipment (after he had spent a week searching his garage for it!). Then there was the rainstorm that weakened the boxes to the point of collapse, followed by the attack of the St. Bernard on the navigator's room. (The navigator was so angry he threatened to quit, so we had to take two days to find a new refrigerator box and help him rebuild his section of the spaceship.)

I'll never forget the day our magical space voyage ended. Apparently, all of our parents met secretly the night before and decided it was time for the spaceship to be dismantled. The lawn under the spaceship was dead, the boxes were caving in after too many dew-filled evenings, and school would be starting in two weeks. We couldn't believe how much debris our spaceship had accumulated over the summer. It took us five full days to rid ourselves of the junk we had collected and to clean up the mess.

What I remember most about my days as captain of our neighborhood spaceship is the wild abandon I experienced. While the spaceship was active, our schedules, our relationships, all of our personal responsibilities fell under the shadow of our imaginary space voyage. Our every waking moment was consumed with the spaceship. By the end of the summer, our parents were frustrated, our friends were angry and jealous, our neighbors were sick of us, and our pets were feeling deprived and rejected because we had ignored them. Our old life had been abandoned for a new life, and we didn't care whether the others thought we used our time wisely or even if they thought we were crazy. We were oblivious to the world around us. It didn't exist. We were children, and for a few short weeks we were allowed to abandon ourselves into the world of our imaginations.

I miss that summer very much. In all the years of my childhood, I was never as alive as I was during those weeks. Every day was vivid, electric, adventurous, invigorating, and exhilarating. Every nerve was standing on tiptoe, every sense was activated, every emotion was alive! My whole being was on call, on alert.

In the summer of 1952, in the unlikely sanctuary of refrigerator and washing machine boxes, I was given my first taste of abandon, my first experience of giving myself over unrestrainedly to an idea larger than myself. God was gifting me, preparing me for that moment when I would bump into Jesus and He would beckon me to come, abandon all else, and follow Him.

❧

JOY BREAKS

For some reason a group of friends got into a discussion about humiliating date experiences. Erik took the prize when he told this story:

"My first date with Kim seemed to be ending perfectly," he said. "After a great dinner and stimulating conversation, we found ourselves seated in a romantic spot on a secluded beach watching the ocean waves roll in."

After a moment, Kim said breathlessly, "I

think we should be closer." Erik, surprised and delighted, happily snuggled closer on the blanket and wrapped an arm around her shoulder.

Kim paused for a moment, then said, "I meant to the water."

Years ago, when Mike started applying to colleges, his father urged him to enroll at the father's alma mater. Mike had planned to attend another school, but finally gave in when he was told, "There's a pretty girl behind every tree!"

One semester later, Mike announced in no uncertain terms that he was transferring to another university. When asked to explain why he was leaving, Mike would only reply, "No trees."

We knew our then four-year-old son, Tony, had been watching a little too much TV after joining him for an afternoon of his favorite cartoons. When a commercial for the Sally Jesse Raphael program interrupted his show, he turned to his mother and said with authority, "Mom, that commercial is wrong. It's not Sally, Jesse, and Raphael. The Teenage Mutant Ninja Turtles are Donatello, Michelangelo, Leonardo, and Raphael."

A Joy-Stealer in the House

Ray could barely contain his excitement. It was Christmas Day, and this nine-year-old boy couldn't wait to tear open those beautifully wrapped presents that bore his name under the tree. Finally, the family was gathered and the joyful celebration began.

Ray quickly grabbed a present, one given to him by his father, and, with childhood expertise, separated the package from its wrapping. Carefully, with anticipation in his heart, he peeled open the box.

Inside was a lump of coal.

Derisive chuckles played accompaniment to Ray's swelling disappointment. Dad had decided to play a gag on his son this year, and he sure thought it was funny.

Ray swallowed hard and tried to keep his spirits up. He reached for another present, also from his father. Enthusiasm tempered a bit, he opened it carefully.

And found yet another piece of coal. Bitterness now replaced the joy Ray had felt only moments earlier. Still, his father laughed.

Unfortunately, the scene repeated itself several times that Christmas morn. Ray's dad had carefully wrapped and placed many presents of coal under the family tree. And each time Ray opened a new lump of coal, he felt the joy of Christmas stolen away from his childlike heart by a Grinch who wore the face of his father.

It's nearly six decades later now. Little Ray has grown up, raised children of his own, served in the military, owned his own business, and finally retired. He has lived a full life and seen many Christmases come and go since the time he was nine. But that coal-filled Christmas remains a vivid memory, and one that still brings pain.

"Dad sure thought that was funny," Ray recalls today, "but, boy, that broke my heart. It hurt this little guy. . . ." Ray's voice trails off, and in an instant you know his father did more than simply play a practical joke on his son. He stole joy from a nine-year-old boy, leaving a scar that still hurts, even sixty years later.

LAUGHTER: JUST THE FACTS

Scientific studies have shown that:

- Laughter reduces stress.
- Laughter is good exercise, stimulating both abdominal and facial muscles.
- Laughter stimulates the immune system, helping combat colds and other illnesses.
- Laughter is aerobic exercise.
- Laughter strengthens your lungs.
- Laughter releases pleasure-enhancing chemicals in your brain.
- Laughter is an effective treatment for depression.
- A good laugh can be like a good massage, relaxing your muscles from head to toe.
- Laughter stimulates creative thinking.
- Laughter is contagious. Are you a carrier?

ABCs for Finding Joy in Life

If you're ever having trouble finding that joyful spark to light up your day, try finding it in these twenty-six places:

1. Attitude adjustments
2. Bible verses
3. Chocolate bars
4. Digging under a rock (like you did when you were a kid)
5. Exercising
6. Family photo albums
7. Grandma's cookin'
8. Heartfelt hugs
9. In a good book
10. Jesus, the source of true joy
11. Kindergarten classes
12. Laughable moments
13. Music
14. Naps
15. Ocean waves
16. Prayer
17. Quiet moments
18. Sunrises
19. Sunsets
20. Toys (electric ones are best!)

21. Ukulele lessons
22. Visiting with visitors
23. Warm puppies
24. Xanadu-like places
25. Yard sales
26. Zoos

❧

SPEAKING OF JOY. . .

"Too many people think God is sorry He ever invented laughter!"

—The Reverend Kent Hummel,
during a 1998 sermon

"It is the heart that is not yet sure of its God that is afraid to laugh in His presence."

—George MacDonald, in *Sir Gibbie*

"All the world is searching for joy and happiness, but these cannot be purchased for any price in any marketplace, because they are virtues that come from within, and like rare jewels must be polished, for they shine brightest in the light of faith and in the services of brotherly love."

—Lucille R. Taylor, as quoted in
Relief Society Magazine

"We have learned that joy is more than a sense of the comic, more than earthly pleasure, and to a believer even more than what we call happiness. Joy is the enjoyment of God and the good things that come from the hand of God. If our new freedom in Christ is a piece of angel food cake, joy is the frosting. If the Bible gives us wonderful words of life, joy supplies the music. If the way to heaven turns out to be an arduous steep climb, joy sets up the chairlift."

—Sherwood Wirt, in *Jesus, Man of Joy*

"Maybe I'm just a cockeyed optimist, but I think life is to be experienced joyfully rather than endured grudgingly."

Luci Swindoll,
in *We Brake for Joy!*

"The habit of always putting off an experience until you can afford it, or until the time is right, or until you know how to do it is one of the greatest burglars of joy. Be deliberate, but once you've made up your mind—jump in."

—Charles R. Swindoll, in *Living on the Ragged Edge*

"Joy is not found in singing a particular kind of music or in getting with the right kind of group or even in exercising the charismatic gifts of the Spirit, good as all these may be. Joy is found in obedience. When the power that is in Jesus reaches into our work and play and redeems them, there will be joy where once there was mourning."

—Richard J. Foster in
Celebration of Discipline

"We must be joyful now. Here. . .within. . . with who we are and what we've got."

—Tim Hansel, in *Holy Sweat*

"The most destitute person
in the world is
the one without a smile."

Zig Ziglar,
in *Zig Ziglar's Little Instruction Book*

"How can I be depressed when you keep acting so positive?"

—from a "For Better or For Worse"
cartoon by Lynn Johnston

A Prayer of
Saint Teresa of Avila[3]

From silly devotions
    and from sour-faced saints,
      good Lord, deliver us!

The Joy Experiments

Experiment #1: Joy Journals

Beginning on a Sunday, chronicle in a notebook or on a yellow legal pad everything that makes you smile. For example, a child's answer in Sunday school, a radiant sunrise, a friend's phone call, a lame joke on late-night TV, a good book, a cozy pet, a lunch with family, a game of football, hot chocolate with marshmallows, a good night's sleep, and so on. Organize your journal by day, and list as many things as you can remember before going to bed.

At the end of your week, review what you've listed and ask yourself these questions:

- What was it about these things that made me smile?
- Why don't I smile more? Or less?
- What can I do this next week to make others smile?
- What do I think makes God smile?

Experiment #2: Overnight Fun-a-Thon

Invite your best friend (a person who may very well be your spouse) to stay up all night on Friday for an overnight Fun-a-Thon. Plan out the whole experience, starting at 10 P.M. Friday and ending at 6 A.M. on Saturday morning. Include anything you two like that makes you laugh, chuckle, smile, or have fun. For example, you might rent a few comedy videos, make a midnight run to the grocery store for chocolate, play goofy games from childhood like Monopoly or Life, practice your karaoke by the stereo, eat more chocolate, invent a bowling alley in your hallway using socks and cola bottles, and, well, you get the idea.

Make the sole purpose of your overnighter simply to have fun and enjoy life with your best friend. When the alarm rings off at 6 A.M., pause for a prayer to thank God for bringing joy into your life, then sleep the day away with a smile on your face.

3

The Fruit of the Spirit Is. . .

Peace

In this world of inescapable horrors, sometimes peace seems unattainable, a phantom we glimpse in the distance that evaporates before we arrive.

Then suddenly, unexpectedly, we are treated to a moment that can only be defined as peaceful. The world still rages, sin still wreaks havoc, our problems haven't gone away or lessened, but in that moment we grasp the truth that Jesus Christ, our Prince of Peace, stands alongside as we face the troubles of the day. May one such moment grace your life today.

ON A QUEST FOR PEACE[4]

We're told this is a true story, so we present it to you as such. It seems there was once a man who was an officer in the British cavalry. A seasoned soldier, and well-trained, he was sent to serve for England in the Crimean War. There he became a part of history as one of the many ill-fated souls involved in the now-famous "Charge of the Light Brigade."

Fortunately, this soldier survived, but the scars on his soul ever after would not heal. The trauma of being in the midst of such carnage made him long for only one thing: peace.

After the war, this cavalry officer resigned his commission, determined not to face battle or war again. He tried to find peace in his native land, but, disillusioned, finally decided England could no longer be the tranquil home he had once known. It was then he decided to leave his home, to travel across the sea and start anew in the fresh, sun-scrubbed skies of America.

Upon arriving, he began a trek to discover the place that would be his home—a place where peace would reign supreme. By the late 1850s, our hero had found and purchased a small farm in the Virginia countryside that had become all he had hoped for. So, he settled in, ready at last to enjoy the remaining years of his life in peace and tranquility.

There was only one problem. The farm on which he had chosen to retire was in an area called Bull Run.

≫

As a high school social living teacher in California, Nancy Rubin often encouraged her students to write "letters" revealing their thoughts and feelings. For one such assignment a student turned her thoughts to peace and war, and a recent visit to a national monument. . .

DEAR VIETNAM WALL[5]

Dear Vietnam Wall,

You are so covered in sorrow that anyone can feel it by a mere glimpse of you. When I saw you I felt so much misery for those who died or are missing, and for those who lost the men engraved in you, that I sat down by your side, and wept quietly for those who cannot. I could not take a single picture of you, because nothing imaginable can capture the incredible emotional experience one experiences at your side. Your picture would have been on the same roll as happy times. You would have made me associate death with cheer and with my friends. You made me think about how insignificant it is to be rich or popular, and cherish the fact that I am alive. I pray that you remain there for centuries to come, to touch other people's souls as you did mine.

—Fifteen-year-old female

NAME OF JESUS, SOFTLY STEALING[6]
(Author unknown)

Name of Jesus, softly stealing
    O'er a world of strife and shame,
Thou canst bring us heav'nly healing,
    O Thou all-restoring Name.

Name of Jesus, Heav'n of gladness,
    Cause our doubts and fears to cease;
Soothe away the aching sadness;
    Name of Jesus, give us peace.

THE WORD ON PEACE

"For unto us a Child is born, Unto us a Son is given; And the government will be upon His shoulder. And His name will be called Wonderful, Counselor, Mighty God, Everlasting Father, Prince of Peace."

—Isaiah 9:6 NKJV

"[Jesus said]
'Peace I leave with you;
my peace I give you.
I do not give to you as the world gives.
Do not let your hearts be troubled
and do not be afraid.' "

John 14:27

"Therefore, since we have been justified through faith, we have peace with God through our Lord Jesus Christ, through whom we have gained access by faith into this grace in which we now stand."

—Romans 5:1–2

"Never pay back evil for evil to anyone. Do things in such a way that everyone can see you are honorable. Do your part to live in peace with everyone, as much as possible. Dear friends, never avenge yourselves. Leave that to God. For it is written, 'I will take vengeance; I will repay those who deserve it,' says the Lord."

—Romans 12:17–19 NLT

"Finally, brothers, good-by. Aim for perfection, listen to my appeal, be of one mind, live in peace. And the God of love and peace will be with you."

—2 Corinthians 13:11

SHALOM!

The Hebrew word for peace used in Scripture is "shalom." Even today, it is commonly used to say good-bye among those of Jewish origin, suggesting that the hearer "go in peace." But, as is always the case when God is involved, there's more to this word than simply a greeting or wish.

Here's how theologian Richard John Neuhaus explains it:

"In both the Hebrew Bible and the New Testament, peace—the *shalom* of God—is tantamount to salvation. It means the bringing together of what was separated, the picking up of the pieces, the healing of the wounds, the fulfillment of the incomplete, the overcoming of the forces of fragmentation by forgiving love. In short, *shalom* is the content of the rule of God, the promised goal of pilgrim hope."

So what kind of *shalom* are you experiencing in life? Perhaps now is a good time to ask God for His *shalom* to reign daily in your life.

&

HOW DO YOU SAY "PEACE"?[7]

In French, you say it "paix."

In Spanish you say it "paz."

In Dutch and Afrikaans you say it "vrede."

In Norwegian you say it "fred."

In Hungarian you say it "béke."

In the Czech language you say it "mír."

In Pig Latin you say it "Eacepay."

At work you say it with a team attitude and in a job well done.

At home you say it with smiles and affection.

At church you say it in the words of the tax collector from Scripture, "God, be merciful to me a sinner!" (Luke 18:13, NKJV)

With enemies you say it in forgiveness.

With loved ones you also say it in forgiveness.

In your heart, you say it by surrender of all to Jesus Christ.

In eternity you say it in a phrase: "Father, I'm home."

❧

PICTURES OF PEACE

What symbols do you associate with peace? A dove? A sunset? Two fingers raised in a "V" shape? The ocean? A rainbow? If you'd like to have physical reminders to seek God's peace each day, try your hand at one of these crafty activities:

Dove Ornament: You'll need scissors, a pencil, and one sheet of white posterboard or heavy paper. Trace the outline of a dove onto your paper. Set or hang this little symbol of peace in a place you're not likely to feel peaceful—for example, hang it from the rearview mirror of your car, or set it on your desk at work. Every time you see it, take a moment to ask God to fill your life with His peace—even if someone does cut you off in rush hour traffic.

Pillow of Peace: Your level of "craftiness" will determine how detailed this craft is—we suggest you keep it easy so you don't lose peace or patience (that's another chapter) in the process. First choose a symbol that represents peace to you. It could be as intricate as a scenic meadow or as simple as the word "peace." Then create a pillow with this image of peace on it. If you're gifted in sewing, you might embroider or cross-stitch your picture on the face of a pillow you've made by hand. Those a bit less talented can purchase a premade pillow and use fabric paints to re-create their image of peace on the pillow. And if you're hopelessly hindered by anything involving a needle, choose fabric crayons to draw your picture of peace on a premade pillow. When your pillow is finished, use it as a place to rest your head when the worries of the world are stealing peace from your heart.

Peace Please! For this simple craft you'll need scissors, light cardboard, a pencil, and the dove you made earlier. Copy the dove onto your cardboard and cut out the shape. This is a small sign you can hang upon your doorknob when you need a few minutes of peace by yourself. You can decorate this placard in any way you like (markers, stickers, doodles) and with any message you like. You might stick with our simple plea of "Peace Please!" or try "Peaceful moment inside—enter quietly," or "Peacefully resting—please don't disturb." Then the next time you're feeling like you could use a few minutes of peace and quiet, hang this notice on your doorknob and close the door. You'll have a few free moments to relax, read, pray, and regain a peaceful heart.

❧

A PRAYER OF MARTIN LUTHER KING JR. (1956)[8]

O God, our Heavenly Father. . . . Keep us, we pray, in perfect peace, help us to walk together, pray together, sing together, and live together until that day when all God's children, black, white, red, and yellow will rejoice in one common band of humanity in the kingdom of our Lord and of our God, we pray. Amen.

PEACEFUL AMERICA?[9]

During a 1952 polio epidemic, 3,152 people were killed by the disease. During a 1990 epidemic of gun violence, 37,184 people in the U.S. were killed by gunfire.

- In 1991 alone, 5,356 children were killed by gunshot wounds.

- In 1992, 1,000,000 crimes with guns were recorded, and 13,000 murders by gunfire were committed.

- The United States has the highest homicide rate in the world, fully four times higher than our closest competitor.

- In an average year, nearly 1,000,000 American teenagers are victims of violent crimes.

- A black teenager is six times more likely to be a homicide victim than a white teenager is.

- Today in the U.S., sixty-five men, women, and children will die due to injuries sustained from handgun fire.

BROKEN CROSSES

As a child in the seventies, I saw a cross,
    upside down and broken, wrapped in
    a circle.
"It's a peace sign," they told me, and I
    tried to believe.
Back then, peace signs spackled across the
    universe,
Sold on T-shirts, necklaces, earrings,
    bandannas, and more.
But the people who held those signs
    always seemed so angry, so ruthless,
    so selfish, so cold.
"That can't be peace," I thought.
As a teenager in the eighties, I saw a
    different cross, this one right side up,
    with a man broken upon it.

"It's Christ," they told me, "and He died
     on the cross to make peace with God
     for you."
Once more, I tried to believe.
It was then I discovered that peace can't be
     found in signs or symbols.
It's not in a necklace or on a T-shirt, or
     pasted to a protester's placard, but in a
     Person, in a relationship,
In the royal family of the Prince of Peace.
Without Him, all we are left with is
     broken crosses, upside down, and
     wrapped in a circle.

A Prayer of
Saint Francis of Assisi[10]

Lord, make me an instrument of Your peace.
Where there is hatred, let me sow love;
Where there is injury, pardon;
Where there is doubt, faith;
Where there is despair, hope;
Where there is darkness, light;
Where there is sadness, joy.

Several years ago, our friends John and Liz Duckworth experienced the heartbreak of losing a newborn child. Katherine Ann Duckworth had the misfortune of being born with a condition called "Trisomy 18"—meaning she was born with a third chromosome. Unfortunately, the condition is almost always fatal.

As John and Liz wrestled with the emotions of dealing with this unexpected trauma, they somehow managed to find peace in the midst of sorrow's storm. Listen now as John recounts his experience during the days after Katherine's birth. . .

KATHERINE
by John Duckworth

Tuesday afternoon we almost lose her. The doctor on duty at Loyola calls us at Central DuPage, reporting Katherine has had a bad spell but rallied. Little by little, her heart is beginning to fail. He wants to know: If her heart stops again, do we want CPR performed on her?

Friends are milling around the room, chatting, as I listen to this stranger ask his life-or-death question. I ask the doctor whether resuscitating Katherine would cause her pain. It could, he says. Feeling she has suffered enough, we tell the doctor that if our baby slips away, not to use such measures to bring her back.

It could happen any time now, we realize. Subconsciously we begin to wait for the phone to ring again, this time with a final message.

I go home for awhile, as I have been doing at night and some mealtimes, feeling alien in my own house. I find myself doing what I never do, flipping my Bible open just to see where it lands, hoping it will land in a place that means something right now.

It opens to 2 Corinthians 4:7–9, 12, 16–18 [NIV]:

"But we have this treasure in jars of clay to show that this all-surpassing power is from God and not from us. We are hard pressed on every side, but not crushed; perplexed, but not in despair; persecuted, but not abandoned; struck down, but not destroyed. . . . So then, death is at work in us, but life is at work in you. . . . Therefore we do not lose heart. Though outwardly we are wasting away, yet inwardly we are being renewed day by day. For our light and momentary troubles are achieving for us an eternal glory that far outweighs them all. So we fix our eyes not on what is seen, but on what is unseen. For what is seen is temporary, but what is unseen is eternal."

Late Tuesday afternoon, Liz is released from the hospital. We trace and retrace the forty-five-minute route between our home and Katherine's, spending as much time with her as we can. We hold her for hours, watching the numbers on the monitors climb and plummet. Whenever they dip too low, alarms sound and a nurse comes running. But Katherine stays alive.

She stays Wednesday to hear the lullaby I wrote for her months ago. She stays Thursday to be held by my parents, who have flown in from Oregon to see their first grandchild and embrace us tearfully. . .But she cannot stay forever. . .

It is Friday, 4 P.M.

Liz and I ride the elevator up to the neonatal intensive care unit. Our parents are back at our house, waiting and praying. There is a room at Loyola in which things like this happen, a room next to the one where Katherine lives. It is a small, windowless room with light green walls and two fold-out chairs in which parents can sleep when they are staying the night. It is to this room that Liz and I go.

We sit on fold-out chairs and wait. I have brought a camera. We have learned this week to take as many pictures as we can.

My heart is in my throat as Katherine is brought in. Dr. Muraskas has prepared us for the possibility that she may have only moments left, but to everyone's surprise she is breathing on her own for the first time.

And for the first time, we see her whole face, without tubes or tape. Her tiny mouth is like a jewel, as silent as always, but pink and perfect. She is unfettered now by electrodes and monitors. There are no fluctuating readouts to stare at in this room, no alarms to dread. There is only an IV stand and a tube connected to her foot, through which she receives nourishment.

She wears the smallest outfit we could find, a newborn size T-shirt with a rabbit on it. It looks like a tent on her miniature frame; her weight has dipped to two pounds, fourteen ounces.

The doctor and nurses leave. Liz holds her first, on a pink and blue and white crocheted blanket. I try to keep my hands from shaking as I take one picture after another. A few times Katherine opens her eyes and we say, "Oh, look!" as if we have seen a shooting star or spouting whale, while in reality we have seen something far more special.

I have used up my film. She is still alive.

My heart thunders in my chest as I drop to my knees and pray aloud, knowing that she could be gone by the time I say amen. "Into Your hands we commend her spirit," I pray, the monumental words sticking in my throat.

She is still with us. We take turns holding her and waiting. . .

The hallways of the great hospital are nearly deserted. We find a small room lined with vending machines. We are too tired to say much as we eat a hastily chosen snack.

We return to the room, and Liz sleeps. I hold Katherine, determined not to doze. She appears to be straining now, gasping for breath. Her heart rate is down to a mere seven beats per minute. I beg God to take her home.

Finally my watch says it is morning. Saturday morning, one week after Katherine's birth. Around 7:30 I lie down as Liz holds our little girl.

I close my eyes. When I open them, it is 8:00.

"I think she's gone," Liz says quietly, looking down at the peaceful bundle in her lap.

Dazed, I go out to get the nurse. She gets

Dr. Muraskas, and they come in. The doctor puts his stethoscope to Katherine's tiny chest. We wait for a long time.

At last he speaks. "She's in heaven," he says simply.

We ask for a few more minutes with her, and are left alone. Liz passes the featherweight body to me, and I hold it to my chest, cradling the precious head under my chin. I touch the softness, the wispy hair, the ebbing warmth I must never forget. I draw a deep breath, and a shuddering sob escapes from somewhere deep inside.

And at that moment, in a place so close yet so far away, on the other side of the door that is this room, a little girl is whole and happy, running and dancing in the Light. There are no tears where she is. No seizures, no defects, no gasping for breath.

I hug what she has left behind. I look through bloodshot eyes across the little room at the brave and beautiful woman who has spent this night as I have, peering into the darkness and sensing the radiant welcome of the Light Himself.

And together, without speaking, we fix our eyes on what is unseen, for that is eternal.

It is why, though we are hard pressed on this bleak March morning, we are not crushed.

And it is why, though our sadness seems unbearable, we are convinced as never before that neither death nor life, nor anything else in all creation, can separate us from the love of God that is in Christ Jesus our Lord.

Nor from our daughter, Katherine.

4

*P*atience

Few qualities of Christian virtue are more needed and desired than patience. The only problem is that patience takes time! You cannot slap a frozen dose of patience in the microwave and have it miraculously appear after two-and-a-half minutes (three in higher altitudes). No, like a garden it must grow, planted first in seed, then being nourished to sprout centimeter by centimeter, inch by inch, until it finally reaches full bloom into our lives.

Our hope is that in this chapter you'll find the encouragement you need to nourish your own garden of patience in the days that come.

A Prayer of William Barclay[11]

O God, my Father, give me patience all
through today.
Give me patience with my work, so that
I may work at a job until I finish it
or get it right, no matter how difficult or boring it may be.
Give me patience with people, so that I
will not become irritated or
annoyed, and so that I never lose
my temper with them.
Give me patience with life, so that I
may not give up hope when hopes
are long in coming true; so that I
may accept disappointment without
bitterness and delay without com-
plaint.
Hear this my morning prayer for Your
love's sake. Amen.

NFL superstar—and Super Bowl champion—Eugene Robinson patiently endured eleven frustrating years as a professional football player before finally winning "the big one." Listen to his thoughts as he reflects on the time he spent waiting for that crowning achievement:

EUGENE ROBINSON:
CHAMPION IN WAITING[12]

Just getting to a Super Bowl—much less winning it—takes incredible endurance on the part of every player and coach on the team. I don't care how talented a team is, how overwhelming it is on offense or defense, that team isn't going to get there without endurance.

Personally, I would never have had a chance to play in the Super Bowl had I not been able to endure some tough times in my career. Don't get me wrong, it's been a great ride for me. I've had some frustrating times in my career, but overall I wouldn't have missed it for anything. I have fond memories of my time as a Seattle Seahawk—even of those seasons where we struggled. But I had to endure eleven years in the NFL in order to have my shot at a Super Bowl championship.

It took a great amount of work and personal sacrifice to reach that goal. . .

The rewards for our perseverance, our hard work—our endurance—were great, both from a professional standpoint and from a spiritual one.

❧

Not knowing how something will end can be so frustrating—especially when there's nothing you can do but wait to see how it turns out! Listen to Amy as she relates what she learned from just such an experience. . .

SURPRISE!

On the evening before my thirtieth birthday, I was stunned to see my husband, Mike, come home with another woman. (OK, so she was just our baby-sitter, Nicole, but I was stunned anyway.)

"You're late!" I snapped. "And why is Nicole here? Don't you know we're supposed to be at Steve and Cindy's right now!"

I'd prepared a meal for our friends who had

just had a baby, and Mike knew he was supposed to be home so I could use the car. By the time he arrived (with the other woman!), the dinner was getting cold, my patience had been exhausted, and I'd spent a good twenty minutes fuming around the kitchen.

Mike simply grinned and said, "Surprise!" Then he calmly added, "Go pack a few things. We're going on an adventure and won't be back until tomorrow morning." Next he turned to our son, Tony, to let him know that Nicole would be staying with him while we were gone.

"Hooray!" said Tony. (He loves Nicole.)

"Forget it," said me. And to prove my point, I started to cry. (You know, one of those hard, red-in-the-face kind of cries—the kind usually reserved for hitting your thumb with a hammer.)

"This isn't what I'd planned," I sobbed.

Mike wrapped his arms around me in a comforting hug. "Trust me," he whispered. "OK?" I dried my tears, gathered my clothes, and reluctantly got into the car.

We dropped off the dinner to our friends, and thirty minutes later were ourselves dining at the nicest restaurant in town. And that wasn't all! We headed to a guest ranch in the foothills of the Colorado Rockies. Mike had rented the honeymoon suite of a beautiful cabin on the river. What's more, he'd sneaked up to the cabin early. As a result of his preparations, a romantic evening of chocolates, sparkling cider, and a cozy fire all awaited me. All I needed to do was wait, and trust that he would arrive in time to celebrate my birthday in a special way.

As I look back on that memory of frazzled patience and honeymoon-style surprises, I realize that I'm not the only one who has almost missed out on a blessing because of being too impatient to wait. Two thousand years ago, Jesus' friends (like me) had to wait in the darkness while Christ prepared a surprise. But instead of bringing home a baby-sitter, Jesus went out to meet his death on a cross.

I imagine that as they watched Jesus marching to his execution, Jesus' followers had some of the impatient, angry, frustrated feelings I had.

"God, this isn't what we had planned! What's going on here?"

"Jesus, we've been waiting for you to set up Your kingdom, not leave us stranded while you are beaten like a common criminal!"

"How can this be happening to Him? To me? How will we ever go on?"

And I imagine God gently wrapping up those people in His arms of love and whispering words of comfort like, "Be patient. Wait. Trust me."

I can't help but think when that stone rolled away from the tomb that first Easter morning that Jesus grinned just a bit and said to the world, "Surprise!" And I picture Jesus crying tears of joy with Mary Magdalene when she realized her waiting was over, that her Messiah had returned to life. I think He must've chuckled with delight when Peter ran to the tomb and found only empty burial clothes.

And, most of all, I'm thankful that He's prepared for me much more than a honeymoon suite in the mountains. On that day when He surprised humanity by defeating death, Jesus made it possible for me to go on a lifetime adventure that leads to an eternal, heavenly home.

If you ask me, that home will be worth the wait.

A Prayer of
Sir Francis Drake
(1540–1596)[13]

O Lord God, when you give to your servants to endeavor any great matter, grant us also to know that it is not the beginning, but the continuing of the same until it be thoroughly finished which yields the true glory.

❧

Two classic fables from Aesop teach us much about the value of patience, so we include for you here The Hare and the Tortoise, *and* The Goose with the Golden Eggs.

The Hare and
the Tortoise

by Aesop

A Hare was once boasting about how fast he could run when a Tortoise, overhearing him, said, "I'll run you a race."

"Done," said the Hare and laughed to himself. "But let's get the Fox for a judge."

The Fox consented and the two started. The Hare quickly outran the Tortoise, and knowing he was far ahead, lay down to take a nap. "I can soon pass the Tortoise whenever I awaken." But unfortunately, the Hare overslept himself. Therefore, when he awoke, though he ran his best, he found the Tortoise was already at the goal.

He learned that "Slow and steady wins the race."

THE GOOSE WITH THE GOLDEN EGGS
by Aesop

Once upon a time a Man had a Goose that laid a Golden Egg every day. Although he was gradually becoming rich, he grew impatient. He wanted to get all his treasure at once. Therefore, he killed the Goose. Cutting her open, he found her just like any other goose, and he learned to his sorrow that "It takes time to win success."

Ten Patience-Enhancers for Everyday Life

Next time you're feeling stressed and your patience is waning, try one of these quick "patience-enhancers" to help reclaim your calm:

1. Pray.
2. Breathe deeply and think of sunsets.
3. Remember God's incredible patience toward you.
4. Eat chocolate. (Might not help, but it'll still taste good!)
5. Pray some more.
6. Give yourself a "time out" and spend ten minutes alone.
7. Read 2 Peter 3:8–9.
8. Put yourself in another person's circumstances.
9. Think eternally. (Is this really going to matter in the long run?)
10. Pray! Pray! Pray!

THEOLOGIAN
LAWRENCE O. RICHARDS
ON PATIENCE[14]:

The New Testament contains many exhortations to be patient. But just what is patience? The Greek word (*makrothymeo/makrothymia*) focuses our attention on restraint: that capacity for self-control despite circumstances that might arouse our passions or cause agitation. In personal relationships, patience is forbearance. This is not so much a trait as a way of life. We keep on loving or forgiving despite provocation, as illustrated in Jesus' pointed stories in Matthew 18. Patience also has to do with our reaction to the troubles we experience in life.

The Bible records the story of Job, a man who, in spite of enduring a host of horrible physical and emotional trials, patiently refused to give up on God. In his beautiful work, The Book of Beginnings, *Dr. Steve Stephens imagines what it might have been like to witness the patient struggles of Job. Listen as he retells a portion of that ancient story here. . .*

THE LAND BARON

Land-Baron could find no comfort. When exhaustion overwhelmed him, night terrors taunted his sleep. During the day unrestrained itching left him crazed. His legs grew thick and swollen until his knees and ankles could not be distinguished. His hard skin cracked and ulcerated, seeping onto the strips of cloth that served as bandages.

The stench forced his wife to keep her distance.

Children stared.

Adults turned their eyes away.

Even the village healer held his breath when he examined the wounds. The healer took Land-Baron's wife aside.

"I wish there was something I could give, but I can do nothing even to ease his suffering. We must protect the village from this horrid sickness. Land-Baron must live in isolation outside the village."

"Must I go with him? Why should I have to suffer because of his disease? Why don't his brothers and sisters take care of him?"

"Your husband will not live long. Try to make his final days comfortable."

That afternoon, Land-Baron moved outside the village. Every step was painful and not even his wife would touch him to help. But his cracked and bleeding lips never complained. He carried his revolting body with a grace.

"Aren't you angry at the Garden-Maker?" His wife spit the words into his face. "Look what you get for all your efforts to be his friend and walk with him."

"I didn't walk with the Garden-Maker to get anything. I did it because of who he is."

"A liar he is. The sky banner to remind us of his care? Look at what he does to his most faithful. He shouldn't care so much."

"There is a reason for all I don't understand. Garden-Maker has an intent. I know he does."

"You pathetic optimist. Cry out to Garden-Maker until you lose your voice. If I were you, I'd curse his name and die."

Land-Baron was silent as he sat in the dusty heat and gritted his teeth against the torment. His wife shook her head and walked back to the village. . .

In spite of the fact that he had now lost everything, Job patiently endured his suffering—so much so that he has since become the ultimate example of human patience, even inspiring the compliment "He (or she) has the patience of Job!"

Curious how Job's patience was rewarded? Read chapter 42 of the book of Job in the Bible to find out for yourself!

THE WORD ON PATIENCE

"The end of a matter is better than its beginning, and patience is better than pride. Do not be quickly provoked in your spirit, for anger resides in the lap of fools."

—Ecclesiastes 7:8–9

"Here is a trustworthy saying that deserves full acceptance: Christ Jesus came into the world to save sinners—of whom I am the worst. But for that very reason I was shown mercy so that in me, the worst of sinners, Christ Jesus might display his unlimited patience as an example for those who would believe on him and receive eternal life."

—1 Timothy 1:15–16

"Bear in mind that our Lord's patience means salvation, just as our dear brother Paul also wrote you with the wisdom that God gave him."

—2 Peter 3:15

"Now may the God of patience and comfort grant you to be like-minded toward one another, according to Christ Jesus, that you may with one mind and one mouth glorify the God and Father of our Lord Jesus Christ."

—Romans 15:5–6 NKJV

"Dear brothers and sisters, you must be patient as you wait for the Lord's return. Consider the farmers who eagerly look for the rains in the fall and in the spring. They patiently wait for the precious harvest to ripen. You, too, must be patient. And take courage, for the coming of the Lord is near.

"Don't grumble about each other, my brothers and sisters, or God will judge you. For look! The great Judge is coming. He is standing at the door!

"For examples of patience in suffering, dear brothers and sisters, look at the prophets who spoke in the name of the Lord. We give great honor to those who endure under suffering. Job is an example of a man who endured patiently. From his experience we see how the Lord's plan finally ended in good, for he is full of tenderness and mercy."

—James 5:7–11 NLT

Sometimes the most difficult person to be patient with is God Himself! Once, after feeling the frustration of seemingly unanswered prayers, Mike wrote this essay he titled:

I PRAYED.
NOTHING HAPPENED.
NOW WHAT?

I once challenged an atheist to pray this simple prayer for seven days: "God, show me the value of prayer. Amen." My "atheist" friend refused the challenge. He was afraid of what might happen. He was worried his prayer might be answered! Then he'd have to change his carefully thought out disbelief—and he didn't want to give God that chance.

Since 95 percent of Americans have experienced answers to prayer[15], that poor atheist had reason to be concerned. Even though he couldn't intellectually admit the existence of God, the truth remains that God does exist and He does answer prayers.

Like the time Reggie White prayed that God would heal torn ligaments in his knee in time for him to play in an important football game for the Green Bay Packers. (God healed him.)[16]

Or the time my church prayed for a boy named Trent. Doctors had discovered an *enormous* blood clot that ran from his leg up into his torso, and they were unable to treat it completely. People in our church took shifts praying for twenty-four hours straight. Next time he went to the doctor, that huge clot was 90 percent gone. Soon after, it disappeared entirely.

When I think of stories like that, sometimes it makes me wonder what I've been doing wrong. Because I know God *does* answer prayer, it makes it all the more frustrating for me when my own prayers *aren't*—and unfortunately that happens more often than I'd like to admit.

I prayed for Nina Brooks for a while. Like Trent, she was a much-loved member of our congregation. She was the sister-in-law of our associate pastor, and a loving wife and mother. And she had a deteriorating liver that was killing her. Her only hope was a liver transplant, but years passed and no liver was available for her.

Nina's condition became critical. The hospital searched frantically for a liver to transplant. And we prayed. Boy, did we pray! Our entire church prayed for weeks, then months, for this woman—much longer than we'd prayed for Trent. Nina slipped in and out of a coma. Then, in spite of our prayers, she died in a hospital bed.

I've found that I'm not the only one whose prayers sometimes go unanswered.

Jeff was in college and a leader in his church's college group when he prayed, "God, let me feel You. Give me some kind of feeling of You to help me know You're real."

Then he waited.

And waited.

And waited some more. Finally, Jeff quit waiting, quit going to church, quit reading his Bible, and quit praying. He never got that "feeling" of God's presence, so he turned his back on Christianity and moved on to something else.

Isaac is a junior in high school. A few years ago, his family took a big leap and opened a small Italian restaurant in town. It was a great hit! Everyone who ate there loved it, and it got excellent word-of-mouth reviews all over town. The only trouble was it wasn't making any money.

Isaac's family poured everything they had into the restaurant. Isaac even worked in the kitchen and filled in as a busboy. All the while Isaac and his family prayed for God to meet the financial needs of the restaurant and their family.

They lasted about a year and a half, then had to file for bankruptcy, sell their house and car to pay as much of their debt as possible, and close the restaurant doors. Isaac's dad now works as a glass installer, and Isaac doesn't understand why God didn't answer their prayers.

At times like these my patience with God wears thin. My soul screams, "God, we prayed! Nothing happened! Now what?" I can't understand why God would work a miracle so Reggie White could play in a football game, and yet do what seems like nothing when the mother of teenagers in my church is left to die, or when a young man turns from God, or when a teenager sees his family go bankrupt.

Oh, I've heard all the standard answers: "Remember, God answers prayers sometimes yes, sometimes no, and sometimes maybe so!" "Remember, God's timing isn't the same as ours!" "Remember, God's going to bring something even better into your life!"

And I've heard all the standard excuses: "You didn't pray long enough." "You didn't pray sincerely enough." "Your prayer was a selfish one." "You must have some sin in your life that blocked your prayer."

Somehow, none of these standard comments give me much comfort—and I'm betting they don't do much for you and Nina Brooks's children either.

So what do I do? I prayed, nothing happened. Now what? It helps me to remember some things.

First, I remember that I'm not alone. In fact, like me (and maybe you too!) Jesus felt the pain of a seemingly unanswered prayer. The Bible reveals in Matthew 26:36–46 that Jesus prayed for deliverance from a "cup of suffering"—that is, His impending death on the cross. (Come to think of it, I'd pray for deliverance from that too!) That request was left unanswered, and Jesus died brutally. . .

. . .then returned to life again having defeated the power of sin and death. Because of that I now have the privilege of knowing God—and praying to Him!

I also remember that God does answer my prayers, just not always in ways that I notice or fully understand. Sometimes instead of asking "Did God answer my prayer?" I need to ask,

"*How* did God answer my prayer?" I prayed for Nina Brooks to be healed. Maybe God's answer in that situation was to bring Nina into His heavenly kingdom where He could give her a new body that's healed for eternity. (See 1 Thessalonians 4:13–18 and Philippians 3:20–21.)

And I remember that prayer isn't just a spiritual version of Santa's toy sack. God never intended my prayers to be wish lists filled solely with my requests for what I think I need. Rather, prayer is a vehicle by which I can miraculously pursue intimacy with the all-powerful God.

So, in that sense, I suppose *something* happens every time I pray. I make contact with eternity. I get a chance to let God know how I feel, to laugh and cry in my Father's presence, and to trust God no matter how life's circumstances turn out.

Perhaps instead of whining, "I prayed, nothing happened," I need to learn how to simply say, "I prayed. That's enough."

Maybe you need to learn that too.

Perhaps the greatest example of patience is seen in the parable Jesus told of the Prodigal Son. As you read it below, remember that, like the father in this parable, God still waits for you to come home too.

THE PRODIGAL SON
(LUKE 15:11–32 NLT)

To illustrate the point further, Jesus told them this story: "A man had two sons. The younger son told his father, 'I want my share of your estate now, instead of waiting until you die.' So his father agreed to divide his wealth between his sons.

"A few days later this younger son packed all his belongings and took a trip to a distant land, and there he wasted all his money on wild living. About the time his money ran out, a great famine swept over the land, and he began to starve. He persuaded a local farmer to hire him to feed his pigs. The boy became so hungry that even the pods he was feeding the pigs looked good to him. But no one gave him anything.

"When he finally came to his senses, he said to himself, 'At home even the hired men have food enough to spare, and here I am, dying of hunger! I will go home to my father and say, "Father, I have sinned against both heaven and you, and I am no longer worthy of being called your son. Please take me on as a hired man.'"

"So he returned home to his father. And while he was still a long distance away, his father saw him coming. Filled with love and compassion, he ran to his son, embraced him, and kissed him. His son said to him, 'Father, I have sinned against both heaven and you, and I am no longer worthy of being called your son.'

"But his father said to the servants, 'Quick! Bring the finest robe in the house and put it on him. Get a ring for his finger, and sandals for his feet. And kill the calf we have been fattening in the pen. We must celebrate with a feast, for this son of mine was dead and has now returned to life. He was lost, but now he is found.' So the party began.

"Meanwhile, the older son was in the fields working. When he returned home, he heard music and dancing in the house, and he asked one of the servants what was going on. 'Your brother is back,' he was told, 'and your father has killed the calf we were fattening and has prepared a great feast. We are celebrating because of his safe return.'

"The older brother was angry and wouldn't go in. His father came out and begged him, but he replied, 'All these years I've worked hard for you and never once refused to do a single thing you told me to. And in all that time you never gave me even one young goat for a feast with my friends. Yet when this son of yours comes back after squandering your money on prostitutes, you celebrate by killing the finest calf we have.'

"His father said to him, 'Look, dear son, you and I are very close, and everything I have is yours. We had to celebrate this happy day. For your brother was dead and has come back to life! He was lost, but now he is found!' "

5

The Fruit of the Spirit Is. . .

Kindness

Pause for a moment right now and answer this question: What is the greatest act of kindness you've ever received from someone? Was it the compassion of a mother? The support of a friend? The encouragement of a neighbor? The generosity of a stranger?

Whatever it was, chances are it not only enriched your life, but made the world a better place for others as well. That's because, like basic mathematics, kindness multiplies, spreading from you to others, who in turn continue spreading it across the globe. May this chapter encourage you to be a multiplier of kindness in the lives of others today, because if it does, we all will feel the benefit.

Novel Advice[17]

Classic American novelist, Henry James, was once saying good-bye to his nephew, Willie. Wishing to give the boy his best parting words of advice, Uncle Henry said this:

"Willie, there are three things that are important in human life. The first is to be kind. The second is to be kind. The third is to be kind."

❧

If I Can Stop One Heart
from Breaking[18]
by Emily Dickinson

If I can stop one heart from breaking,
    I shall not live in vain;
If I can ease one life the aching,
    Or cool one pain,
Or help one fainting robin
    Unto his nest again,
I shall not live in vain.

COMPASSION
by Dr. Harold J. Sala

World War II was winding down when Bob Pierce visited a mission school and orphanage run by a group of German sisters near the Tibetan border. While he was there, Pierce noticed a little girl hunched at the bottom of the cold, stone steps. The little girl was obviously undernourished and lacked proper clothing for the cold climate. The child could not have been more than nine or ten, yet her gaunt little face and coal-black eyes reflected as much suffering as some endure in a lifetime.

Deeply concerned, Pierce asked one of the sisters about her. "Oh," she replied, "she comes and sits there every day. She wants to come to school. But we have no room."

The reply did not satisfy him, so he said, "Surely one child won't make that much difference. If she wants to come so badly, could you not make room for just one more?"

The sister turned to Pierce and said, "We have made room for 'just one more' time and time again. We have already four times the number of children we were originally prepared to care for. We have stretched our food as far as it will go. I myself am feeding three others out of my rice bowl, as are all the other sisters. If we do not draw the line somewhere, there will not be enough rice to keep the children we already have alive. We simply cannot take one more child!"

The brutal reality of the situation hit home, but Pierce did not want to accept it. "That is crazy, ridiculous!" he said. "A child cannot come asking for help and be turned away at the door. Why isn't something being done?"

Without saying anything, the sister walked over and swooped the little girl up in her arms. Walking over to Pierce, she deposited the girl in his strong arms and said, "What are you going to do about it?"

That incident led to the founding of World Vision—an organization that has helped feed and clothe thousands of boys and girls. Pierce did what I think you would have done. He dug into his own pocket and gave the sister enough money to buy rice for the little girl. . .

A sister's question founded a great organization. "What are you going to do about it?" It is the question every person must face. When you think of the needs of all the world, you are overwhelmed, but if you can think of the one person outside your gate and face the question, "What am I going to do about it?" you will find that the darkness is driven back at least one step. The needs of people come one at a time; eventually every person must answer the question: "What am I going to do about it?"

❧

TEN RANDOM ACTS OF KINDNESS YOU CAN DO THIS WEEK

1. Scratch or massage a family member's back.
2. Serenade your mother (she won't mind if you're a little off-key).
3. Leave coins for kids in gumball machines.
4. Let someone behind you in line go ahead of you.
5. Buy lunch for the car behind you in the fast-food drive-thru lane.
6. Compliment every person you come in contact with during a day.
7. Tell someone the good news of Jesus'

death and resurrection.

8. Write thank-you cards to your friends just to tell them you appreciate their friendship.

9. Laugh at someone else's jokes.

10. Share your chocolate (OK, just a small piece).

❧

The extraordinary kindness of Mother Teresa toward the sick and dying of the world still stands as a monument years after her death. What was her secret? Perhaps it was in this prayer that she prayed every day:

A Prayer of Mother Teresa of Calcutta, India[19]

Dearest Lord, may I see you today and every day in the person of your sick, and whilst nursing them minister to you.

Though you hide yourself behind the unattractive disguise of the irritable, the exacting, the unreasonable, may I still recognize you and say "Jesu, my patient, how sweet it is to serve you."

Lord, give me this seeing faith, then my work will never be monotonous. I will ever find joy in humoring the fancies and gratifying the wishes of all poor sufferers.

O beloved sick, how doubly dear you are to me, when you personify Christ; and what a privilege is mine to be allowed to tend you.

Sweetest Lord, make me appreciative of the dignity of my high vocation and its many responsibilities. Never permit me to disgrace it by giving way to coldness, unkindness, or impatience.

And, O God, while you are Jesus my patient, deign also to be to me a patient Jesus, bearing with my faults, looking only to my intention, which is to love and serve you in the person of each of your sick.

Lord, increase my faith, bless my effort and work, now and for evermore.

KESHIA, KINDNESS,
AND THE KKK[20]

Eighteen-year-old Keshia Thomas awoke with a purpose on her mind that warm summer day in 1996. This was the day the infamous Ku Klux Klan was holding a rally near her home in Ann Arbor, Michigan. Many people who opposed the Klan's racist views had planned to gather and march in protest of the organization. A young black woman herself, Keshia was determined to join them.

The protest started off peacefully as crowds of people flooded the streets, waving signs, singing, and shouting to the opposition. Suddenly, almost from nowhere, a white man appeared and flaunted his T-shirt which supported racism and praised the efforts of the KKK. At first people passed him by, but before long his obnoxious sneer and taunting apparel angered many of Keshia's fellow demonstrators.

Without warning, several protesters surged from the ranks of the march and surrounded the lone KKK supporter. Deluging him with kicks, fists, and signs, they quickly overpowered the white man, knocking him down and angrily beating him while he was on the ground.

Nearby, Keshia watched in horror as the terrible unkindness of the KKK supporter sparked an even greater unkindness in the demonstrators. In a selfless act of kindness for her "enemy"—and risking injury herself—Keshia flung herself into the fray. Shouting for the crowd to stop, she dropped to the ground and covered the man, using her own body as a shield to protect him from further injury.

The stunned crowd was silent for a moment. Then, one by one, they slowly rejoined the march and walked harmlessly away. Keshia's risky act of kindness toward an enemy had saved the man—and the day.

❧

THE WORD ON KINDNESS

"Blessed be the LORD, For He has shown me His marvelous kindness in a strong city!"
—Psalm 31:21 NKJV

"Be kind and compassionate to one another, forgiving each other, just as in Christ God forgave you."

—Ephesians 4:32

"Therefore, as God's chosen people, holy and dearly loved, clothe yourselves with compassion, kindness, humility, gentleness and patience. Bear with each other and forgive whatever grievances you may have against one another. Forgive as the Lord forgave you."

—Colossians 3:12–13

"What is desirable
in a man is
his kindness."

Proverbs 19:22 NASB

"Make sure that nobody pays back wrong for wrong, but always try to be kind to each other and to everyone else."

—1 Thessalonians 5:15

A KIND WORD?

The old joke goes something like this:
   A man was on a business trip away from

home at Thanksgiving, and unable to get back in time to spend the holiday with his family. Discouraged and missing his wife and children, he stopped at a diner to eat his lonely Thanksgiving dinner.

"What'll you have?" the waitress asked.

"Just a slice of pumpkin pie and a few kind words," he replied.

Soon after, the waitress returned, placed his order on the table, and turned to walk away.

"Wait a minute!" the man called. "What about my kind words?"

Checking to make sure the cook was out of earshot, the waitress leaned over and whispered, "Don't eat the pie."

❧

TEN RULES FOR GETTING RID OF THE BLUES[21]
by James S. Hewett

Ten rules for getting rid of the blues: Go out and do something for someone else, and repeat it nine times.

The ultimate act of kindness is the one we often have the most difficulty with: forgiveness. We would do well to learn from the example of Corrie Ten Boom. . .

A LETTER FROM CORRIE TEN BOOM TO THE MAN WHO BETRAYED HER FAMILY TO THE NAZIS[22]

Today I heard that most probably you are the one who betrayed me. I went through ten months of concentration camp. My father died after nine days of imprisonment. My sister died in prison too.

The harm you planned was turned into good for me by God. I came nearer to Him. A severe punishment is awaiting you. I have prayed for you, that the Lord may accept you if you will repent. Think that the Lord Jesus on the Cross also took your sins upon Himself. If you accept this and want to be His child, you are saved for eternity.

I have forgiven you everything. God will

also forgive you everything, if you ask Him. He loves you and He Himself sent His Son to earth to reconcile your sins, which meant to suffer the punishment for you and me. You, on your part have to give an answer to this. If He says: "Come unto Me, give Me your heart," then your answer must be: "Yes, Lord, I come, make me your child." If it is difficult for you to pray, then ask if God will give you His Spirit, who works the faith in your heart.

Never doubt the Lord Jesus' love. He is standing with His arms spread out to receive you. I hope that the path which you will now take may work for your eternal salvation.

❧

An Unforgiving Servant (Matthew 18:21–35 ncv)

Then Peter came to Jesus and asked, "Lord, when my fellow believer sins against me, how many times must I forgive him? Should I forgive him as many as seven times?"

Jesus answered, "I tell you, you must forgive him more than seven times. You must forgive him even if he does wrong to you seventy-seven times.

"The kingdom of heaven is like a king who decided to collect the money his servants owed him. When the king began to collect his money, a servant who owed him several million dollars was brought to him. But the servant did not have enough money to pay his master, the king. So the master ordered that everything the servant owned should be sold, even the servant's wife and children. Then the money would be used to pay the king what the servant owed.

"But the servant fell on his knees and begged, 'Be patient with me, and I will pay you everything I owe.' The master felt sorry for his servant and told him he did not have to pay it back. Then he let the servant go free.

"Later, that same servant found another servant who owed him a few dollars. The servant grabbed him around the neck and said, 'Pay me the money you owe me!'

"The other servant fell on his knees and begged him, 'Be patient with me, and I will pay you everything I owe.'

"But the first servant refused to be patient. He threw the other servant into prison until he could pay everything he owed. When the other servants saw what had happened, they were very sorry. So they went and told their master all that had happened.

"Then the master called his servant in and said, 'You evil servant! Because you begged me to forget what you owed, I told you that you did not have to pay anything. You should have showed mercy to that other servant, just as I showed mercy to you.' The master was very angry and put the servant in prison to be punished until he could pay everything he owed.

"This king did what my heavenly Father will do to you if you do not forgive your brother or sister from your heart."

In his play, Debtor's Prison, *our friend Paul Lessard has written a beautiful allegory of Christ's kindness to us—and our response to Him. We're honored and grateful to be able to include Paul's dramatic expertise as the closing for this chapter.*

DEBTOR'S PRISON
by Paul Neale Lessard

Summary: Three men are in debtor's prison. In three scenes we hear their stories and come to an understanding of our own positions as debtors before God.

CHARACTERS

Duncan—A longtime resident of the prison, he is hard and gruff, aloof, always cool and unflustered.

William—Another longtime resident, he shows more emotion and is somewhat softer than Duncan.

Terry—A newcomer to the prison.

Prison Guard

Narrator—Person offstage who introduces the scenes.

A prison cell. One-inch dowels of varying lengths, painted black, and nailed to a 2 x 6-inch board placed across the front of the stage (downstage right and left) will serve as a grim reminder of the location. Downstage center is where the bench should sit. A table and two chairs are set stage right and a bunk bed is set at an angle, opening up to the audience, just to the left of center stage.

THE SCRIPT
"DEBTOR'S PRISON"
SCENE 1

(As the audience arrives, have a cassette of blues-type music playing in the background. Reserve a seat in the middle of the auditorium for Terry. When it's time for the show to begin, fade out the music and bring up the lights on Duncan and William playing Checkers. Terry enters, wearing drab, tattered clothing and carrying a rolled-up blanket, and sits in the reserved seat.)

Narrator: (Offstage) In mid-18th century
England, Europe, and even in Colonial

America, it was not uncommon for men to be imprisoned with no hope of release as a result of bad debts. To be consigned to a debtor's prison, as it was called, was to be forever condemned.

William: (Sits up suddenly and moves a checker, jumping three of his opponent's checkers.) Ha! King me!

Duncan: (Waving his fist in William's face) I'll king you all right.

William: (Pointing at the board) C'mon Duncan, king me. I didn't even cheat this time.

Duncan: (Disgusted) After all these games, you finally admit you cheat?

William: (Ignoring Duncan's comment) Right here, make this checker a king.

Duncan: (Reluctantly crowning the checker) Just because you're getting the first king doesn't mean you've won the game.

William: (Gleefully) Not yet, anyway!

(They continue to play, absorbed in the game. At this point the guard enters from the back of the auditorium carrying a dirty piece of paper. It has a list of names with descriptions on it. He stops about halfway up, looks around, spots Terry, and comes to the end of Terry's row. He looks back at his paper and then up at Terry, points to him, and motions for him to come. Terry slowly stands up, looks helplessly around, and points to his chest. The guard nods. Terry, looking defeated, makes his way to the guard, who then escorts him to the stage. No words are exchanged. Escorted by the guard, Terry enters stage right behind the table. The guard then leaves. Terry looks at the two men, who seem oblivious to his presence, and then crosses to the bottom bunk to put his blanket there.)

Duncan: (Without looking up) I wouldn't put anything there if I were you.
(Terry stops, straightens up, and reaches to put the blanket on the top bunk.)
William: (Clears his throat.) Ahem. . .
(Terry stops once again and turns around to face the men, who still don't look up.)
Duncan: (As he moves a checker) I should think this one can sleep on the bench. What do you think, William?
William: Suits me fine. Under the window, maybe?
Duncan: (With an air of finality) Under the window on the bench.

William: It's best really; the last chap didn't last too long sleeping on the floor.

(Terry slowly crosses and places his blanket on the bench. He takes off his jacket and puts it on top of his blanket.)

Terry: It doesn't much matter where I sleep. I won't be here long.

William: (With mock amazement) Won't be here long? (They both turn to look at Terry.) Don't you know where you are, boy?

Terry: Sure I do; I'm not a fool.

Duncan: (Back to his Checkers game) Then don't talk like one.

William: This is the Dunsmire Debtor's Prison.

Duncan and William: (In unison) No one ever leaves.

Terry: No one?

Duncan: (Contemplating his next move) At least not alive.

Terry: (Disbelieving) What? Are you telling me that no one ever pays off their debts?

Duncan: (Looking at Terry) If you couldn't take care of your debts on the outside, what makes you think you'll be able to do it in here?

Terry: The jailer said that I could work off my debt.

Duncan: Don't build your hopes on a jailer's empty promise.

William: From our first day, we both tried to work our way out of this prison. It makes the most sense at the start. But after a while you come to realize that you owe so much and you earn so little.

Duncan: (Back to his Checkers, shaking his head) I'm surrounded by naive fools.

Terry: But my family! I have to get out. My wife and children cannot live with my brother the rest of their lives. (Pause) All it took was two bad crop years, and I was unable to pay the rent on the land we farmed. We had nothing to eat; how could they expect me to pay any rent? If only he could've given me another chance. (Turning away) I'm not a bad person.

Duncan: (Sharply) None of us is. It's just not enough to be good. You didn't measure up financially. None of us did, or we wouldn't be here.

William: (Wishfully, playing an invisible violin) I had a music shop. Violins, violas, cellos, and double basses. (Looking at his hands) I made instruments that brought music to the whole of England. And

Duncan, well, he was a baker. His pastries, buns, and sweetmeats were the talk of Surrey. What did you call your bakery, Duncan?

Duncan: Duncan's Doughnuts.

William: He was famous even in London, where I lived.

Terry: I'm a farmer. Or was. . .

William: Well, you can learn another trade here. Like making shoes,

Duncan: or saddles,

William: or baking,

Duncan: or games of Checkers,

William: or license plates.

Duncan and Terry: License plates?

William: It's experimental. No one really knows what they're for. (Shrugs) But, same as you, we fell upon hard times and were unable to pay our creditors, so we ended up in here.

Terry: (Kneels beside his blanket and begins to arrange it like a bed on the bench.) Well, I'll not be in here long. If I work hard and long enough, I know I can pay off my debts and get out of here!

William: (Nodding his head slowly) I wish it were true.

(Silence as Terry arranges his bed.)

Duncan: (Jumping two checkers) King me. It's your turn, William, but I believe the game may be mine this time.

William: (Turning back to the game) Maybe, but I'm still ahead of you 2,346 games to 1,998.

Duncan: So you've had a couple of good years. I've got plenty of time to catch up.

(Fade to black. Fade in blues music while stage is dark. Fade out blues as lights come up for Scene 2.)

SCENE 2

Narrator: (Offstage) Terry committed himself to working hard. It was not uncommon for him to put in 15- or 16-hour days, seven days a week in his efforts to pay off the debt that led to his imprisonment. Finally, after his first full year in the Dunsmire Debtor's Prison, he asked the jailer for a review of his work. Terry wanted to know how far along he was in paying off his debt.

(Scene opens with Duncan and William playing Checkers again. However, William is lying on the top bunk, with his hand under his head, looking at the ceiling and humming. Duncan is engrossed in the game. He has only one red checker left, and the black checkers are doubled—all William's pieces are kings. Duncan is making blowing noises in his frustration as he tries to figure out his next move.)

William: Give up, Duncan.
Duncan: Never!
William: (Sitting up on one elbow) You have one checker left. I have all kings. Admit it, you're defeated.
Duncan: More time—I need more time.
William: Well, that's the one thing I do have plenty of. . .
(Terry walks in slowly. He's wearing a very worn bandanna around his neck. He sits down in William's chair and stares numbly at the floor. Duncan and William exchange glances.)
William: (Sitting up and hanging his legs over the edge of the bed) Well?
(Silence from Terry.)
Duncan: (Back to the game) See, I told you,

you cannot work your way out of here.

Terry: (Slowly looking up at Duncan and then William) Rags, it's all just rags. (Stands up, rips bandanna from his neck, and holds it up, clenched in his fist.) He said all I've done is like filthy rags. My work amounts to nothing. I'll be here until I die! I owe more than when I came.

Duncan: Spare me the theatrics. We told you before not to expect so much. In debtor's prison you can't pay for your own debts.

Terry: (In anger and frustration, sweeps the checkerboard onto the floor, looks into Duncan's face.) OK, if you have all the answers, then tell me—who can?

Duncan: (Standing up face-to-face with Terry, hostile) If I knew the answer to that question, do you think I would be standing here wasting my days in your company? (Gesturing to William) Or his?

William: (Gently, to break the tension) Someone able, who cares enough about you to pay your debt, that's who.

Duncan: (Glaring at William) And none of us knows anyone like that! (Turns away and begins to pick up the checkers.)

William: (To Terry) When Duncan's business

began to fail, he asked his father-in-law for money. His father-in-law is the Duke of Hazards. He lives in the southern part of England and is a very wealthy man. The duke never cared for his daughter's marriage to a commoner, so instead of helping him, he allowed Duncan to be put in prison.

Duncan: Poor timing, really. I was about to enter into a partnership with an old Scottish farmer named Ronald. We were intending to open a new shop and name it after him: Ronald McDonald's. We were going to use my fresh bread and his meat to make a special sandwich named the McDuncan or Big Dunc or something like that. But, when my father-in-law would not help me out. . . (His voice trails off.)

Terry: (Looking at Duncan) I'm sorry Duncan. You shouldn't be in here.

William: None of us should. I would still be in my shop if my landlord had not decided he wanted to put a tavern there. He began to raise the rent until I could no longer pay. By the time I left, he had seized all my instruments. I had nothing with which to pay the back rent, the taxes, or the suppliers for my trade.

Terry: (Sitting back down) What're we going to do? We all owe so much. I owe so much. Two years' back rent on the land and a year of food from my brother. It would take a king's ransom to cover my debts. And I don't know anyone with that kind of money.

Duncan: Well, I do, and it doesn't make my situation any better.

Terry: My wife has written to all our relatives asking them for their help, but they all are in the same situation we are. Except, of course, they've not landed in here.

William: (Jumping down from the bed) Wait a minute, chaps, there was a fellow here once who told me a remarkable story. He had heard of a nobleman in the north of England who was known to despise debtor's prisons. The story goes that the nobleman, whom I think was supposed to be a prince, liked to pay off prisoners' debts and thereby secure their release.

Terry: (Looking up) I think I've heard that story before. (Thinking) The nobleman was. . .the Duke of Northumberland.

Duncan: So what's the rest of the story?

William: (Beginning to realize the importance
of his story) Apparently a prisoner some
years ago wrote a letter to this duke.

Duncan: (Intently) And then?

William: They say that after a month or so this
prisoner packed up and left.

Terry: (With new hope) He left alive!

William: Pardon me?

Terry: You said, "No one leaves alive." This
man left alive.

Duncan: William! Why have you not remembered this?

William: I never really believed it could be
true—thought it an old prisoner's wishful
tale. Until now. (Shrugging his shoulders)
Besides, when I first heard the story, you
were ahead of me by 186 games in
Checkers. I wanted a chance to catch up.

Terry: This is our only hope.

Duncan: (With more life and energy than
we've seen from Duncan so far) We must
contact this gentleman immediately.

William: I'll get the phone.

Duncan and Terry: The what?

(Fade to black. Blues music up. Fade music out
as lights come back up for Scene 3.)

(Scene opens with Duncan and William playing Checkers once again. There is a smattering of kings on the board, but the game is even. Duncan and William are somewhat distracted, however, and occasionally glance toward Terry. Terry is lying on the bench but gets up and crosses to the door, looking out the window. He paces nervously and looks uneasy.)

Narrator: (Offstage) Duncan, Terry, and William did get a letter out of the prison to the Duke of Northumberland. They explained how their debts were impossible to pay on their own, and they asked for mercy. After that, all they could do was wait.

Duncan: (After William moves a checker) Now William, my friend, are you sure that's the move you want to make?

William: (Innocently) Why, whatever do you mean?

Duncan: It just seems like a rash move, and I'm quite willing to let you make that move again, if you feel for some reason that's not your best choice.

William: That's so considerate of you, Duncan.

But I think I'll let my marker stay as it is.

Duncan: (He moves a checker, growls.) This game requires no skill whatsoever; it's just a matter of luck!

William: (Jumps four checkers.) Ahh. . .got lucky again. King me. . .

Terry: (Impatiently) Why has the Duke of Northumberland taken so long to reply? You would think he would at least acknowledge our letter.

Duncan: You're sure it was the Duke of Northumberland that was in the story?

Terry: (Somewhat irritated) Yes, yes. We've been through this before. (Pause) At least I think it was Northumberland.

Duncan: And William, you're certain that he paid the way for this other prisoner to be released?

William: (Impatiently) Yes, Duncan. Yes.

Terry: (Sitting up) Someone's coming.

(They look at the edge of the stage expectantly, and the guard enters with a rolled-up sheet of paper.)

Guard: Terry Coppersmith?

Terry: (Nervously) Yes?

Guard: I have a message from. . .(looking at the edge of the scroll) the Duke of

Northumberland. (He hands the scroll to Terry.)

(Terry crosses to the front of the table holding the rolled-up message. Duncan and William stand up and come to either side of him. Terry should be right in front of William's chair. Terry holds the paper nervously.)

Duncan: (Impatiently) Don't wait all day, man, open it!

William: (Gently) Open it, Terry. Read to us what it says.

(Terry carefully unrolls the sheet of paper. He reads the first line silently and then sinks into the chair with a sense of hopelessness.)

Terry: (Reading from the letter) "Kind Sirs: On the 31st of May this past year, the Duke of Northumberland died. . ." (He lowers the letter into his lap and looks at the floor.)

Duncan: (Disbelieving) He's dead?

Terry: (Weakly) He's dead.

Duncan: (Frustrated, sits down at the table as he speaks.) Why did I let myself believe that someone else could ever cover my debts? No one cares, and we can no longer help ourselves. It's hopeless.

William: (Taking the letter and holding it at arm's length to read it) "Kind Sirs: On the 31st of May this past year, the Duke of Northumberland died. During the duke's life, he secured the release of many a ward from debtor's prisons all across England. When the duke was a boy. . ." (Continues reading to himself, muttering occasionally.)

Terry: (Quietly) I'll never see my family again.

Duncan: (To himself with disgust) I do not know why I allow myself to get caught up in these irresponsible schemes.

Terry: I'll be here the rest of my life. In this room.

Duncan: (As he studies the game, all business) William, the game awaits.

William: (Growing excited) Listen to this! "But with the death of the Duke of Northumberland comes hope for many in the debtor's prisons of England. For the entire estate and holdings of the duke are being used to secure the release of all prisoners at the Dunsmire Debtor's Prison." (Yells joyfully) His death secures our release. Duncan, Terry, we're free! (Begins playing an imaginary violin and waltzes around the stage, humming, full of joy.)

Duncan and Terry: (Blankly) The Dunsmire Debtor's Prison?

William: (Stopping for a second, pointing to the letter) The release is secured for all prisoners at the Dunsmire Debtor's Prison. (Comes behind the table and slaps both of them on the back.) My friends, we'll be free; we ARE free! Our debt is paid! (He looks down at the game, pauses, then jumps a checker twice.) I believe this game is mine, Duncan. (He begins to waltz some more, playing the violin.) I shall have a new store and make nothing but the finest instruments of exotic woods from around the world.

(As Terry stands up to deliver his lines, Duncan looks down at the game and quietly begins to reset.)

Terry: (Grinning broadly) I'll find a new farm. This is a new start, and I'll not waste it.

(William's dancing has brought him to the door of the cell; he stops.)

William: The door is open. (Looking out) Prisoners are running all over out there. Duncan, Terry, let us gather our possessions and go home! (Both he and Terry quickly begin to gather up their things.)

Terry: (Laughing) I can't wait to see the look on my wife's face.

William: (Laughs) The look on her face? I can't even remember what my wife looks like! (William and Terry both laugh again. As they turn to head for the door they notice Duncan, who is studying the checkerboard.)

Duncan: (To himself) The key is not to sacrifice too many, too soon. Let the other player be aggressive.

William: (Gently) Duncan?

Terry: The door is open; we're free to go.

Duncan: (Firmly, not harshly, not mournfully) No one is interested in paying my debt. It's my concern. No one cares.

William: Ah, but that's no longer true, my friend. The death of one man has brought freedom for all.

Terry: Your debts are paid, Duncan. You're free. You have a fresh start. (They move toward the door) Come with us. Come! (Terry walks offstage.)

William: (Hesitates) Duncan, please come.

Duncan: I think not. You go.

William: Duncan. . .(Pauses, then sadly) Good-bye. (Turns and leaves)

Duncan: (Sighs as he pushes aside the checker-board) I think I'll take up Chess.

(Fade to black. Blues music comes up and then fades out.)

6

The Fruit of the Spirit Is. . .

*G*oodness

Look out your window today. What do you see? Is it sunny? Is the wind rustling through the leaves on the trees? Is snow falling gently outside your door? Do robins sing or crickets "crick," or raindrops pitter-patter on your porch? Are children playing down the street? Does the moon loom brightly on a starlit night? Is there anything of beauty wrapped up in your little world?

Of course there is, and each little "present" is yet one more proof of the goodness of God. May this chapter encourage you to notice God's goodness today—and inspire you to imitate His goodness in your life, thoughts, and actions as well.

THE GOLDEN AX

The classic fable goes like this. . .

Once there was a poor but honest woodcutter. Every day he would take his ax of steel, march into the forest and chop enough wood to buy bread for his family.

One day he was chopping down an old oak tree on a river bank when he accidentally knocked the precious ax into the swirling depths of the river.

"What will I do?" wailed the poor man. "I've lost my ax! How will I feed my children?"

Just then a water fairy rose from beneath the surface of the water. "Why are you sad?" she asked. The woodcutter explained how he had clumsily lost his ax.

Feeling pity, the water fairy dove into the river, and came up with an ax of purest silver. "Is this your ax?" she asked.

For a moment the poor woodcutter thought of all the things he could buy with the silver in that ax, then he shook his head and said, "No, my ax is merely made of steel."

The fairy dove under water again, and returned with an ax made of finest gold. "Is this your ax?" she asked as she laid it on the river bank. Again the woodcutter said no—denying a fortune beyond his wildest dreams.

A third time the fairy dove deep into the river, and this time she returned with an ax of steel. "Ahh," said the woodcutter, "that is my ax."

"Take it then," said the fairy, "and because you are a man of good character, you may take the other two axes as a gift from the river." And so the woodcutter had newfound riches to buy all kinds of good things for his family's future.

❧

GOODNESS IN AMERICA: A STATISTICAL EVALUATION

Consider this:

More than half of Americans say they will: "drink and drive if I feel that I can handle it" (56 percent); "cheat on my spouse—after all, given the chance he or she will do the same" (53 percent); "do absolutely nothing [at work] one full day in every five" (50 percent).

In spite of the fact that roughly 90 percent of Americans say they "truly believe in God," 84 percent of those same people say that they would willingly "violate the established rules of their religion."

Seventy-four percent of Americans say they will "steal from those who won't really miss it."

Sixty-four percent of Americans say they will "lie when it suits me."

Only 30 percent of Americans would be willing to die for God or their religious beliefs; and 48 percent of Americans say that they have no beliefs they would be willing to die for.

By contrast, for the salary of a professional sports super-star, about one out of every four Americans would do the following: "abandon their church" (25 percent); "abandon their entire family" (25 percent); "become a prostitute for a week or more" (23 percent).

Our young people are not unaffected by the lack of personal character exhibited in our society. According to a recent study by the Josephson Institute of Ethics, one-third of all college students believe that "in today's society, one has to lie or cheat at least occasionally in order to succeed." And, even though 78 percent of high schoolers said cheating on exams is "always wrong," 61 percent admit having cheated within the past year.

There is good news, however. In the area of personal character, faith in God does make a difference. In a landmark, nonreligious study of Americans' private morals, researchers James Patterson and Peter Kim came to this conclusion[23], "Religious people are more moral."

According to Patterson and Kim, religious Americans are:

- better workers;
- more truthful;
- less likely to abuse drugs;
- less likely to commit a petty crime;
- less likely to be swayed by peer pressure into doing something they know is wrong;
- more committed to their families; and
- more willing to risk their lives for their beliefs.

A "What's Inside Counts" Recipe

In life—as is often the case in cooking—it's the good stuff on the inside that really counts. Treat yourself to delicious reminders of that truth by baking your own batch of these tasty, good-stuff-on-the-inside cookies!

¾ cup powdered sugar
½ cup butter, softened
1 tablespoon vanilla
1 ½ cups flour
½ teaspoon salt
chocolate kisses, chocolate chips, raisins,
    or other small sweets

Mix powdered sugar, butter, and vanilla. Add in the flour and salt. If mixture is too dry, mix in 1 to 2 tablespoons of milk.

Take about a tablespoon of dough in your hand and mold it around the candy, raisin, or other treat you've chosen. Form a ball with none of the inside goodie showing.

Place cookies about an inch apart on an ungreased cookie sheet. Bake at 350 degrees about 12 minutes. Cookies will not be brown on the tops, but will firm up as they cool.

Makes about 24 cookies.

❧

A GOOD MAN IS HARD TO FIND[24]

Nate "Tiny" Archibald has always been one of the good guys. His effortless dribble, crisp passes, and soft-touch shooting ability made that much obvious. Whether he was tearing up the basketball courts at the University of Texas-El Paso, or knocking down jump shots on the parquet floor of the Boston Garden, it was clear this guy was good—very good.

In fact, during a fourteen-year career as a professional basketball player, Tiny Archibald was one of the best. From his point guard position, he routinely lit up the boards with both his scoring and deft passing. In 1972–73, he became the only player in NBA history to lead the league in both scoring (averaging 34 points a game) and assists (averaging 11.4 per game) in the same season. As a member of the 1981 Boston Celtics, he helped propel his team to an NBA championship. Six years after he retired, he was easily inducted into the NBA Hall of Fame.

Tiny Archibald showed on the court that he was a good player, but it was off the court where he showed he was also a good person. In his heyday as a basketball legend, Tiny never forgot where he came from: the streets of New York City. During his off-seasons, Tiny always made it a point to return home, running basketball clinics for kids, coaching amateur teams, and even buying equipment for young people.

A few years after his basketball retirement, in 1989, he went home to stay, taking a job as a junior high health and physical education teacher at an inner-city public school in Harlem, New York. While many of his pro basketball Hall of Fame peers have gone on to lucrative careers in business, broadcasting, coaching, and the like, Tiny shunned that big-money kind of work to make a better, longer-lasting investment in people.

"People wonder why I'm back here," Mr. Archibald explained during his ninth year as a professional educator, "but I just love kids. . . . These kids need positive people to take an interest in them."

And so Nate "Tiny" Archibald—NBA legend—has decided to be one of those people.

It's said that a good man is hard to find. But not if you look at the P.S. 175/ I.S. 275 school in Harlem. You'll find him in either the Health or P.E. classroom, sharing a bit of himself with America's future.

꒦

SPEAKING OF GOODNESS. . .

"Goodness is stronger than evil;
  love is stronger than hate;
  light is stronger than darkness;
  life is stronger than death;
  victory is ours through him who loved us."
                    —Bishop Desmond Tutu,
              as quoted by Mary Batchelor in
                  The Doubleday Prayer Collection

"You are never weary, O Lord, of doing us good. Let us never be weary of serving You."
                    —John Wesley,
              as quoted by Horton Davies in
                  The Communion of the Saints

"It is a good thing to do good deeds. It is an even better thing to be a good person."
                    —Anonymous

"I was on the football field at our local high school the other day, where my son was running cross country. As I watched these boys and girls, I was preoccupied with recent problems. I also remembered my cross-country days twenty-five years ago and naturally breathed a prayer of thanksgiving. The prayer was something like, 'Lord, thank you so much that I'm not running cross country any more.'

"Then I sort of loosened up a bit and looked around me. The sky was blue; the leaves were yellow; the air was crisp. I began to enjoy the beautiful day. I forgot my problems and quietly thanked God for the beauty of the world around me. My spirits lifted as I began to appreciate the goodness of God, right there in the middle of the football field."

—John Yates, in a sermon entitled,
"An Attitude of Gratitude"

"Someone has said that the difference between a mere optimist and a Christian optimist is that the former lives by the principle that life is good and the latter by the principle that God is good."

—Robert C. Shannon,
in *1000 Windows*

"Do all the good you can, to all the people you can, in all the ways you can, as often as ever you can, as long as you can."

—Charles Haddon Spurgeon,
as quoted in *Draper's Book of
Quotations for the Christian World*

*"Mere acquaintance with a good man
is a powerful antidote to evil."*

George MacDonald, in
The Miracles of Our Lord

"Books and friends should be few, but good."
—Anonymous

"The Christian is in a different position from other people who are trying to be good. They hope, by being good, to please God if there is one; or—if they think there is not—at least they hope to deserve approval from me. But the Christian thinks any good he does comes from the Christ-Life inside him. He does not think God will love us because we are good, but that God will make us good because He loves us."

—C. S. Lewis in
Mere Christianity

"Good will toward all men is a result of the invasion of the supernatural! A state of good intention with 'heartiness and cheerful consent' toward all mankind, if Webster is correct. A state of heart so extraordinary as to be un-heard of, except by those who have been hurled out into the place of joyful, utter despair with themselves, where they are finally allowing Jesus Christ to be Himself in them!"

—Eugenia Price, in
Christianity Today, volume 1

THE WORD ON GOODNESS

"How great is your goodness [God], which you have stored up for those who fear you, which you bestow in the sight of men on those who take refuge in you."

—Psalm 31:19

"What can I give the LORD for all the good things he has given to me? I will lift up the cup of salvation, and I will pray to the LORD. I will give the LORD what I promised in front of all his people."

—Psalm 116:12–14 NCV

"To this end also we pray for you always, that our God will count you worthy of your calling, and fulfill every desire for goodness and the work of faith with power, so that the name of our Lord Jesus will be glorified in you, and you in Him, according to the grace of our God and the Lord Jesus Christ."

—2 Thessalonians 1:11–12 NASB

"Great is the LORD
and most worthy of praise;
his greatness no one can fathom. . . .
The LORD is gracious
and compassionate,
slow to anger and rich in love.
The LORD is good to all;
he has compassion
on all he has made."

Psalm 145:3, 8–9

"The LORD is my shepherd; I shall not want. He makes me to lie down in green pastures; He leads me beside the still waters. He restores my soul; He leads me in the paths of righteousness for His name's sake.

"Yea, though I walk through the valley of the shadow of death, I will fear no evil; For You are with me; Your rod and Your staff, they comfort me.

"You prepare a table before me in the presence of my enemies; You anoint my head with oil; My cup runs over.

"Surely goodness and mercy shall follow me all the days of my life; And I will dwell in the house of the LORD forever."

—Psalm 23 NKJV

❧

No exploration of goodness is complete without the story that Jesus once told of a despised, half-Jew, half-Gentile man whose actions revealed the goodness in his heart.

THE GOOD SAMARITAN
(LUKE 10:29–37)

He asked Jesus, "And who is my neighbor?"
In reply Jesus said: "A man was going down

from Jerusalem to Jericho, when he fell into the hands of robbers. They stripped him of his clothes, beat him and went away, leaving him half dead. A priest happened to be going down the same road, and when he saw the man, he passed by on the other side. So too, a Levite, when he came to the place and saw him, passed by on the other side. But a Samaritan, as he traveled, came where the man was; and when he saw him, he took pity on him. He went to him and bandaged his wounds, pouring on oil and wine. Then he put the man on his own donkey, took him to an inn and took care of him. The next day he took out two silver coins and gave them to the innkeeper. 'Look after him,' he said, 'and when I return, I will reimburse you for any extra expense you may have.'

"Which of these three do you think was a neighbor to the man who fell into the hands of robbers?"

The expert in the law replied, "The one who had mercy on him."

Jesus told him, "Go and do likewise."

There's no telling the difference a word of encouragement can make in a person's life. To paraphrase Proverbs 25:11, a few good words, appropriately chosen, are as beautiful as apples of gold in settings of silver. Don't believe it? Maybe Shelly can convince you.

By all accounts, Shelly was just another average student back in her high school days. In fact, she hardly did anything to warrant more than the passing attention of her classmates and teachers. That near-anonymous high school career earned Shelly one memory about her youth. "I got very few compliments," she recalls.

If you were to look at her today (and you probably have), you'd think she wasn't telling the truth about that. You see, she's widely regarded as one of America's most beautiful—and talented—actresses. She's starred in one hit movie after another, performing opposite to Hollywood's most-desired leading men. She's been featured on the cover of America's most prominent magazines, has earned millions with her talent, and has managed to sustain an enduring, successful career as an actress.

Still, in high school, she never dreamed

she'd obtain the kind of success and accolades that would eventually be hers. In fact, she was really just an average kid hungry for a compliment or two.

Which leads us to Shelly's second memory of her teen years: a few good words spoken by an encouraging teacher. Five words in all, not many—but enough.

"I think you have talent," the teacher said. And young Shelly listened, treasuring those words, making them her own.

Today, megastar Michelle Pfeiffer smiles when remembering her teacher's brief affirmation, saying "I never forgot it. It's amazing how something [like that] can alter the direction of your life. I came to feel very confident [about acting] because of that one comment."

A few good words literally changed Michelle Pfeiffer's life. Maybe a few good words from you can do the same thing for someone else too. You'll never know unless you try.

TOZER ON GOODNESS[26]

In his classic work, The Knowledge of the Holy, *theologian A. W. Tozer explains more about what God's goodness really means with these thoughtful insights:*

"The goodness of God is that which disposes Him to be kind, cordial, benevolent, and full of good will toward men. He is tenderhearted and of quick sympathy, and His unfailing attitude toward all moral beings is open, frank, and friendly. By His nature He is inclined to bestow blessedness and He takes holy pleasure in the happiness of His people.

"That God is good is taught or implied on every page of the Bible and must be received as an article of faith as impregnable as the throne of God. It is a foundation stone for all sound thought about God and is necessary to moral sanity. To allow that God could be other than good is to deny the validity of all thought and end in the negation of every moral judgment. If God is not good, then there can be no distinction between kindness and cruelty, and heaven can be hell and hell, heaven.

"The goodness of God is the drive behind

all the blessings He daily bestows upon us. God created us because He felt good in His heart and He redeemed us for the same reason."

❧

GOODNESS KNOWS

Goodness knows that sometimes the greatest thing in the world is a smile from a child,
So Goodness laughs a lot.
Goodness knows it's easier to break a child than to mend one,
So Goodness handles with care.
Goodness knows that everyone deserves a second chance,
And sometimes a third and fourth chance too.
Goodness knows we all need friends in this world,
So Goodness is determined to be friendly.
Goodness knows that only people count,
So Goodness never counts out people.
Goodness knows life is sometimes lonely,
But we are never alone.
And when the sorrows of life are left unexplained, it's still not too much to bear,
For we can trust that Goodness knows.

Recently Mike was asked to share at our church about his experience with God's goodness during difficult times. Here is what he had to say:

GOD IS GOOD.
ALL THE TIME.

Ever notice that life is often more like a soap opera than a sitcom? In a sitcom, minor crises appear, then are neatly resolved within thirty minutes (including commercials). The happy characters hug at the end, and all is well.

Soap operas, on the other hand, are chock-full of long, drawn out tragedies and emotional extremes. Illnesses last for years, marriages break up with regularity, plane and car wrecks throw characters into comas, evil people scheme and hurt the good folk. And the drama never seems to end until an actor decides to leave the show.

Although our family has more than its share of happy, sitcom times, in the last two years we've also seen some of those soap opera moments crop up in our lives. Like the fall of 1997 when, after seven years of secondary infertility, Amy miraculously got pregnant and then suffered a miscarriage. Or last February, when I held my quietly sobbing son as he was crying himself to sleep because a much-anticipated adoption had just fallen through, and now he knew he would be a big brother to no one. Or last month when a slipped disc in Amy's back became so debilitating she couldn't even sit up to take pain medicine.

But probably the longest running soap opera in our family has been a chronic stomach illness I've had since December of 1996. This illness causes me to feel some level of nausea every day. I call it my own personal "morning sickness." After a routine gallbladder surgery, I started throwing up several times a day and had trouble keeping any food down. I went to a doctor who told me it was all in my head; I should either get over it or learn to live with it. Several weeks—and 25 lost pounds—later, I found a new doctor, but it took him about six months to finally discover what was wrong with me, and more than a year before we arrived at a treatment that's at least 80 percent effective.

Needless to say, persistent nausea has affected every area of my life. I didn't work for three months in 1997, and am now only able to work about thirty hours a week. I've had to drop out of volunteering for youth ministry, cancel projects, withdraw from social events and more. Currently, I'm on a battery of medicines that allows me to function almost normally, and for that I'm grateful. But I am not healed.

Many people have prayed for my healing. The elders of this church have prayed for me twice. Friends and family and many of the kids in our youth group still continue to pray. Two people I trust and respect told me they'd seen visions of God bringing miraculous healing to my body.

But still, I'm not healed. I can't say why God has chosen not to heal me at present, but I can say that even when I'm kneeling in front of the toilet for the umpteenth time, God has also chosen never to leave me.

During the last two years, I've had ample opportunity to examine my faith in Jesus, and I've discovered a few things.

First, I've realized that I do not serve God because of what He does for me, but because of who He is. It doesn't matter if I feel slighted or ignored or wronged by the circumstances God has allowed in my life. What matters is that He is God. Period. End of story. That's why, like Job, I'm trying to become a man who can honestly say, "Though He slay me, yet will I serve Him."

Second, I've learned I must completely trust Jesus for even the smallest details of human accomplishment. I can't take a shower unless Jesus keeps my stomach from churning. I can't work unless Jesus allows me to overcome my daily "morning sickness" and get out of bed. I can't ride to the grocery store unless God protects me from the all-too-frequent carsickness episodes. And, in a way, that's very freeing. My life is not in my control. That means I must truly trust in Him to direct my days. And when I say "God willing, I'll do thus and so," I really mean it now!

Finally, I've seen confirmed the truth that God is good. All the time.

In sickness, He's given me faithful friends who've mightily cared for me and my family. In sorrow, He's given me the comfort of a loving wife and son. In weakness, He's given me strength through His Spirit. In poverty, He's provided miraculous funds. In helplessness, He's given me peace. In hopelessness, He's granted power to persevere.

Like King David in Psalm 27:13 (NIV), I stand before you today to report:

"I am still confident of this:
I will see the goodness of the LORD
in the land of the living."

And, as the very next verse instructs, I intend each day simply to:

"Wait for the LORD;
be strong and take heart
and wait for the LORD."

Thank you.

7

The Fruit of the Spirit Is. . .

Faithfulness

Over a dozen years ago, we sat choosing songs to be sung at our upcoming wedding ceremony. Although we each tossed out ideas, there was only one that we both knew from the start had to be included: "Great Is Thy Faithfulness."

That old hymn which proclaims "Great is Thy faithfulness, O God my Father. . ." had proven to be true in our separate lives—and continues to be true in our lives together today. If only we were as faithful in everyday life as God is with us! May this chapter encourage us all to strive for that goal.

OPENING THOUGHTS FROM
BROTHER LAWRENCE[27]

"When we are faithful to keep ourselves in His holy presence, it begets in us a holy freedom."

❧

IN CASE YOU FORGOT. . .[28]

In case you forgot, we thought you should know that in many parts of the world, it just isn't safe to live as a faithful Christian. Consider these events that happened as recently as 1998:

June, 1998. The Saudi Arabian government arrested seven Christians. Their "crimes" were distributing Christian literature and showing the *Jesus* film. In a country that tolerates no religion other than Islam, those are high crimes. One of those arrested was Yolai Aguilar, a woman from the Philippines. Though nine months pregnant, it's believed she was tortured and forced to reveal the names of other Christians in Saudi Arabia. Evidence suggests the other six detainees were also tortured with the same intent.

In this same month, a group of American

Christians visited Chiapas, Mexico, to deliver seven metric tons of food along with medical supplies to refugees in the area. While there, they were attacked by a mob of nationals who threw rocks and sticks at the Americans' bus while shouting "Foreigners get out!" Fortunately, no one was injured.

September, 1998. "All the Christians in the Maldives"—about fifty believers—were reportedly placed in prison. The Maldives, a small island off the coast of India, is overwhelmingly Muslim. Arrested Christians were allegedly detained in small cells and forced to observe Islamic customs such as reading the Koran and reciting Islamic prayers five times a day.

Also in September, 1998, Christians in Laos were reportedly forced to drink boiling water until they revealed the names of other Christians who were giving them Bibles. Those newly exposed Bible-couriers were subsequently detained and also allegedly abused physically.

So, in case you forgot, being a Christian isn't always a painless endeavor for many of your brothers and sisters around the world—and even here at home in America.

Why not take a moment to pray for the faithful who are suffering for Christ today?

Top Ten Ways to Express Your Faithfulness to God

1. Worship no one other than God.
2. Don't make or worship idols of any kind.
3. Don't misuse God's name.
4. Observe the Sabbath, and keep it holy.
5. Give honor and respect to your parents.
6. Don't murder.
7. Don't commit adultery.
8. Don't steal.
9. Tell the truth.
10. Be satisfied with what you have instead of enviously desiring what someone else has.

(Paraphrased from Exodus 20:1–17)

CHRISTIAN FAITHFULNESS IN AMERICA: A STATISTICAL PICTURE

During 1998, pollster George Barna surveyed over 1,000 U.S. adults to find out their attitudes toward religion. A few of his findings[29]:

More than eight of every ten Americans (83 percent) rate "religious faith" as something that's very important in their lives.

Eighty-two percent of those surveyed reported they were "Christian," but only 50 percent said they were "absolutely committed to the Christian faith." And only 39 percent were "born-again Christians."

Forty-three percent of those surveyed attend church at least once during a given week.

Nearly two-thirds of those surveyed report they did not read their Bible (other than at church) in the previous week.

Four out of five Americans say they prayed in the previous week, but less than half report participating in other religious activities (such as reading the Bible or attending church) during that same week.

Three out of four adults (77 percent) do not attend Sunday school.

Eighty-two percent of adults do not attend a small group at church.

Only one in four of those surveyed say they've volunteered at church.

Also in 1998, the Yankelovich Partners polled 1,000 American adults, asking whether or not they engaged in religious conversation at work. Turns out [30]:

An overwhelming majority of workers (70 percent) are talking about Jesus and faith in God at the water cooler, in the boardroom, on the auto assembly line, in retail stores, and wherever else they happen to clock in.

Half of Americans (50 percent) talk about religion with their coworkers at least once a month.

Women are twice as likely as men to talk about God at work during any given month. Twenty-nine percent of these ladies broach the topic more than once in a month, whereas only 15 percent of men do the same.

Of those who bring God to work, 85 percent also attend church each week, and 76 percent say they attend church at least once a month.

Surprisingly, however, more than half (54 percent) of those talking about faith also report that they "rarely or never" go to church. That suggests that: 1) Non-Christians are talking about God; and/or 2) Christians are talking about their faith, but not acting on it by joining a community of believers.

Lieutenant John Blanchard was determined to be faithful to his country as he served in the U.S. Army during World War II. And at the same time, he longed to be faithful to his heart, a heart which had been stirred just weeks prior while taking a break at a Florida library.

Looking through a book from the stacks, John spotted one that looked interesting. Opening the pages he noticed not what the original author had written, but the gracefully stroked notes softly penciled in the margins. He read a few of those notes, and then a few more. In this anonymous note author, he sensed he'd found a kindred spirit. He was irresistibly drawn to the person who expressed such thoughtful, meaningful prose— even if it was only in the margin of a book.

Flipping to the front page, John found a name to attach to the words he was already beginning to treasure: Miss Hollis Maynell. She had apparently been the previous owner of the book, donating it to the library when she was done with it.

After an exhaustive search that took several weeks, John finally located an address for Miss Maynell in New York City. The day before his unit was to journey overseas for combat in World War II, he wrote a letter to Hollis Maynell, introduced himself, told how he'd come to contact her, and asked if she'd be willing to trade letters with him while he was gone. For the next thirteen months, Miss Maynell did just that, faithfully corresponding with this soldier fighting her country's battles. And with each new letter John received from her, he felt the flush of attraction to this mysterious, yet inwardly beautiful woman.

At one point, John asked for her photograph, but Hollis Maynell declined, telling him that if he really cared for her, it wouldn't matter what she looked like. Finally the time came when John returned home to the United States, and the pen pals set a date for a meeting. On the appointed day, John was to carry a book and wait for her at 7 P.M. at Grand Central Station in New York.

Her letter informed, "You'll recognize me by the red rose I'll be wearing on my lapel."

So, on the appropriate day, at the appropriate time, John Blanchard found himself standing in Grand Central Station, peering intently at passersby for a glimpse of the rose that would identify the woman he had come to love. Here's how he describes what happened next:

A young woman was coming toward me, her figure long and slim. Her blonde hair lay back in curls from her delicate ears; her eyes were blue as flowers. Her lips and chin had a gentle firmness, and in her pale green suit she was like springtime come alive. I started toward her, entirely forgetting to notice that she was not wearing a rose. As I moved, a small provocative smile curved her lips. "Going my way, sailor?" she murmured.

Almost uncontrollably I made one step closer to her, and then I saw Hollis Maynell.

She was standing almost directly behind the girl. A woman well past forty, she had graying hair tucked under a worn hat. She was more than plump, her thick-ankled feet thrust into low-heeled shoes. The girl in the green suit was walking quickly away. I felt as though I was split in two, so keen was my desire to follow her, and yet so deep was my longing for the woman whose spirit had truly companioned me and upheld my own.

And there she stood. Her pale plump face was gentle and sensible, her gray eyes had a warm and kindly twinkle. I did not hesitate. My finger gripped the small worn blue leather copy of the book that was to identify me to her. This would not be love, but it would be something precious, something perhaps even better than love, a friendship for which I had been and must ever be grateful.

I squared my shoulders and saluted and held out the book to the woman, even though while I spoke I felt choked by the bitterness of my disappointment. "I'm Lieutenant John Blanchard, and you must be Miss Maynell. I am so glad you could meet me; may I take you to dinner?"

The woman's face broadened into a tolerant smile. "I don't know what this is about, son," she answered, "but the young lady in the green suit who just went by, she begged me to wear this rose on my coat. And she said if you were to ask me out to dinner, I should go and tell you that she is waiting for you in the big restaurant across the street. She said it was some kind of test!"

❧

Advice on Faithfulness from Charles Dickens to His Son Henry[32]

As your brothers have gone away one by one, I have written to each of them what I am now going to write you. You know that you have never been hampered with religious forms of restraint, and that with mere unmeaning forms I have no sympathy. But I most strongly and affectionately impress upon you the priceless value of the New Testament, and the study of that book as the one unfailing guide in life. Deeply respecting it, and bowing down before the character of our Saviour, as separated from the vain constructions and inventions of men, you cannot go very wrong, and will always pre-serve at heart a true spirit of veneration and humility. Similarly, I impress upon you of the habit of saying a Christian prayer every night and morning. These things have stood by me all through my life, and remember that I tried to render the New Testament intelligible to you and lovable by you when you were a mere baby. And so God bless you. Ever your affectionate Father.

❧

FROM THE MOUTHS OF BABES

Not long ago, the children in our church were learning about baptism. Their teachers carefully explained how this rite of Christianity was endorsed by Jesus, and that Christians have been faithfully performing this rite of faith ever since.

After the lesson, one preschool teacher, Dee Carillo, was tickled to hear her four-year-olds request more information about the topic, though she did have to stifle a chuckle when little Nathan and Jack confused baptism with personal hygiene and asked, "Teacher, how old were you when you were Bathtized?"

THE WORD ON FAITHFULNESS

"I will sing of the LORD's great love forever; with my mouth I will make your faithfulness known through all generations. I will declare that your love stands firm forever, that you established your faithfulness in heaven itself. . . . The heavens praise your wonders, O LORD, your faithfulness too, in the assembly of the holy ones. . . .

"O LORD God Almighty, who is like you? You are mighty, O LORD, and your faithfulness surrounds you."

—Psalm 89:1–2, 5, 8

"Let love and faithfulness never leave you; bind them around your neck, write them on the tablet of your heart. Then you will win favor and a good name in the sight of God and man."

—Proverbs 3:3–4

"If we are not faithful, he will still be faithful, because he cannot be false to himself."

—2 Timothy 2:13 NCV

"Be faithful, even to the point of death, and I will give you the crown of life."

—Revelation 2:10

"Unless you are faithful in small matters, you won't be faithful in large ones. If you cheat even a little, you won't be honest with greater responsibilities. And if you are untrustworthy about worldly wealth, who will trust you with the true riches of heaven? And if you are not faithful with other people's money, why should you be trusted with money of your own?"

—Luke 16:10–12 NLT

❧

The greatest opportunity for faithfulness is found simply in keeping these traditional vows made to a spouse during a wedding ceremony. . .

FAITHFUL VOWS

Minister (to bride and groom): I now charge you both, as you stand in the presence of God, to remember that true love and faithful observance of your marriage vows are required as the foundation of a successful marriage and the establishment of a happy home. Without these there can be no real marriage and the home which you will endeavor to establish will be a vain effort. Keep the solemn vows you are about to make. Live with tender consideration for each other. Conduct your lives in honesty and in truth. And your marriage will last. Your home will endure. The marriage bond will be a blessing to you, and you will be a blessing to others. This should be remembered as you now declare your desire to be wed. Now, do you (Groom) take this woman to be your wedded wife? And do you solemnly promise, before God and these witnesses, that you will love her, comfort her, honor and keep her in sickness and in health, and that, forsaking all others for her alone, you will perform unto her all the duties that a husband owes his wife, until God, by death, shall separate you?

Groom: I do.

Minister (to the Bride): Do you (Bride) take this man to be your wedded husband? And do you solemnly promise, before God and these witnesses, that you will love him, comfort him, honor and keep him in sickness and in health, and that, forsaking all others for him alone, you will perform unto him all the duties that a wife owes her husband, until God, by death, shall separate you?

Bride: I do.

Minister: Since it is your desire to take each other as husband and wife, please join your right hands, face each other, and repeat after me, before God and these witnesses, the marriage vow.

(To the Groom) Repeat after me: "I (Groom's name), take thee (Bride's name) to be my wedded wife, to have and to hold from this day forward, for better or for worse, for richer or for poorer, in sickness and in health, to love and to cherish till death do us part, according to God's holy ordinances and, thereto, I pledge thee my faith.

(To the Bride) Repeat after me: I (Bride's name), take thee to be my wedded husband, to have and to hold from this day forward, for better or for worse, for richer or for poorer, in sickness and in health, to love and to cherish till death do us part, according to God's holy ordinances and, thereto, I pledge thee my faith.

(To all present) Now, those whom God has
joined together, let no man put asunder.

❧

FAITHFUL VOWS,
PART 2

Remembering her first date with a specific man
Sylvia shares, "He confessed that he was married, but that his wife was in a nursing home
permanently, having suffered a severe stroke
years ago. *Nice try*, I thought. *I happen to know
the lady; she's in my book club.*"[33]

We wryly laugh at Sylvia's experience, thinking what a cad this man must be to lie so
brazenly. Yet would we have had different feelings for him if his story were true? Would we
have justified his seeking a date with a young
woman if his wife were, in reality, wasting away
in a nursing home?

Those wedding vows, the ones that go, "In
sickness and in health," or the part that says,
"till death do us part." How seriously do people
take these? Surely there are many who, like
Sylvia's date, think nothing of the vows they
once made. When times get tough, it's time to

move on. But a vow is a vow, and the faithful do not make vows lightly—or forget them quickly.

Morris Forman is such a man. He easily remembers meeting his wife Eve over fifty years ago. Back in the days when there were rules to courting, Eve was bold enough to knock on the door of Morris's New York home and tell him he'd been "recommended" to her by her cousin.

"A woman calling on a man, boy, that never happened in those days," Morris recalls. "I was so lucky."

Morris married bold young Eve and they've been married fifty years now. Morris loves his wife just as much, even after all these years. Even after all the changes that have occurred. And what sad changes they are.

Morris and Eve were unable to have children, so Eve became "Aunt Eve" to all the neighborhood kids. Now Eve is certain a stuffed doll is the child she never had and clings to it constantly.

Eve was once a bookkeeper, with a mind so bright she was able to quickly multiply three-digit numbers in her head. That same mind now can't tell her fingers how to use a spoon.

The long walks they once enjoyed are now taken down the halls of a nursing home. You've probably guessed. Eve has Alzheimer's. So while Morris recalls the Eve that once was, the marriage that once was, the love that once was, Eve remembers nothing. This cruel disease has stolen her memories.

Yet Morris is faithful. He visits Eve every day. He holds her hand. He talks to her quietly. He holds a weekly sing-along for Eve and the other residents. He holds his wife close and tells her he loves her, because he still does. As Morris puts it, "Just because someone has a disease doesn't mean the love is gone."[34]

ℭ

Ever wonder what would happen if we sports fans applied our attitudes about church faithfulness to our favorite teams? It might look something like this treatise from an anonymous fan:

WHY I'VE STOPPED SUPPORTING MY TEAM
by an Ex-Sports Fan

1. Whenever I go to a game, they ask for money.

2. The other fans don't care about me.
3. The seats are too hard.
4. Coach never visits me.
5. The referee makes calls I don't agree with.
6. Some of the games go into overtime and make me late for dinner.
7. The band plays songs I don't know.
8. I have other things to do at game time.
9. My parents took me to too many games when I was growing up.
10. I know more than the coaches anyway.
11. I can be just as good a fan at the lake.
12. I won't take my kids to a game either. They must choose for themselves which teams to follow.

❧

THANK GOD
FOR FAITHFUL PASTORS![35]

Sure, it looks like an easy job. A pastor only works Sundays, right? And spends the rest of the week golfing. And gets paid to read the Bible. And is widely respected, well loved, and living happily ever after with the church family, right?

Don't count on it. Although a pastor's life can include those elements, a recent study by *Leadership* magazine revealed pastors often serve faithfully in a thankless job.

Consider:

On average, a pastor labors about fifty-five hours per week on the job.

A pastor typically works more evenings and weekends than most other American professionals do.

Pastors invest roughly eleven hours a week in preparation for a Sunday morning sermon that usually only lasts thirty to forty-five minutes—and is mostly forgotten within an hour after church ends.

Over half of America's pastors have never had any time management training, but are expected to juggle a dizzying array of administrative and pastoral duties without any complications whatsoever.

Nearly half of our pastors say they're working too hard—yet nine out of ten pastors still say they find satisfaction in the work they do.

Why not take a moment today to thank God—and your pastor—for pastors.

❧

Recently Mike had the opportunity to chat with renowned pastor and author Max Lucado. During their conversation, Max shared a bit about how he had learned the importance of being faithful in prayer while stationed as a missionary in Brazil. Here's what Max had to say:

MAX LUCADO ON BECOMING FAITHFUL IN PRAYER[36]

Max L.: The prayer life for me really came to life when I was a missionary in Brazil. Our church was a missionary church; it was a small, struggling, storefront congregation. And a man came to be a part of our church who became a Christian through a Pentecostal movement in Brazil.

He was a wonderful Christian man who had a drug problem. And he came to Rio de Janeiro, Brazil, right out of a drug rehab center. And this Pentecostal drug rehab center turned that man into a prayer warrior. This is incredible, Mike, but it's the truth. He was required in that rehab center to spend three hours each day on his knees—from six to seven in the morning, from twelve to one at lunch, and then from six to seven in the evening.

I remember he told me, "Whether we prayed or not was up to us, but we had to be on our knees." And he came to our church—I think the Lord sent him our way—and his first question to us was "Why don't you pray?" And we said, "Well, we pray. I mean. . .you know." So he said, "Why don't you pray?" And so I would meet him every afternoon for an hour of prayer in our little church building.

Mike N.: Can you share his name?

Max L.: Yeah, I can. I honestly don't remember his last name. It's been over twelve years since I've seen him! But his first name was Abel. Wonderful, nice-looking, young man. Fiery, fiery man. Real committed to Christ.

And so the two of us would get down on our knees in that little church building, get on the concrete floor, and he would rock back and forth on his knees and he would pray. He'd say, "Oh, Lord, equip the church. Lord, equip the church. Equip the church." He'd just say it over and over again. He was just so passionate in his prayers. And with time, that became contagious to me. I think I learned what James means when he says, "The earnest prayers of a faithful man availeth much." For I saw in him earnest prayers.

I would love to have a more earnest prayer life! Mike, in my life, prayer is the single most difficult discipline. I love God and there's something in me that would rather do things for God than talk to God. I'm not by nature a mystical, devotional person. I like to do things. And so it's a challenge for me to have a faithful prayer life, but I know God loves me and He's not mad at me. He just wishes I would slow down and turn things over to Him. And that's what I think you achieve through prayer.

ॐ

PARTING THOUGHTS FROM CHARLES W. COLSON[37]

"God calls me to be faithful, not successful. The end result is in His hands, not mine."

8

Gentleness

It's true that we live in a harsh world, but it's also true that gentleness invades that harshness with its own kind of beauty. We see it in the way a mother cradles a newborn baby, in the eyes of a father roughhousing with a preschooler, in the silence of a setting sun, in the affectionate caress of a lifetime lover and friend, in the peace that settles during an anxious prayer, and in a thousand ways more.

Yes, gentleness is invading your world today. The only question is whether or not you've joined the revolution.

GENTLE JESUS, MEEK AND MILD
by Charles Wesley

Gentle Jesus, meek and mild,
Look upon a little child;
Pity my simplicity,
Suffer me to come to Thee.

Lamb of God, I look to Thee;
Thou shalt my example be:
Thou art gentle, meek and mild;
Thou wast once a little child.

Fain I would be as Thou art;
Give me Thine obedient heart:
Thou art pitiful and kind;
Let me have Thy loving mind.

Loving Jesus, gentle Lamb,
In Thy gracious hands I am;
Make me, Saviour, what Thou art,
Live Thyself within my heart.

In his powerful book, Choosing to Live the Blessing, *John Trent shares memories of the gentle touch of his mother's hands—and how that gentleness shaped who he is today. Listen as he shares it now with you. . .*

PICTURES OF MY MOTHER
by John Trent

Like Robert Cormier, when I think of my childhood, my thoughts stumble upon a thousand pictures of my mother's hands. But for different reasons.

She couldn't untie knotted shoestrings, button winter coats, iron shirts, or straighten ties. Simple things, but she couldn't do them. From my earliest memory, my mother's hands were bent and twisted with rheumatoid arthritis. The world wouldn't think them beautiful, but they were beautiful to me and to my brothers. They became, over the years, a symbol of her love for us.

Because of the pain in those twisted joints, my mother could not grab your hand. She never took your hand and shook it. When she took it, she touched it gently, squeezing just a part of it. Holding on to you softly. Then releasing you from her touch.

That's how she held on to each of us boys. Tenderly. Softly. With great affection and warmth. And yet loosely.

I remember when [my twin brother] Jeff and I turned ten, she dressed us up in our finest sports coats and clip-on ties. Her hands weren't strong enough to tie a real knot, and there was no man around the house to do it. She took us to a fancy restaurant, and at dinner she made sure we knew that we were now "young men" and were expected to act as such. After dinner, she gave us each a dollar and told us, to our amazement, that we were to leave the tip. It was a rite-of-passage for us, for from that day on we were expected to take more and more responsibility. My mother never paid another bill or left another tip when we were with her. She would slide us the money under the table, and we would assume that duty. We were learning, through her soft hands and gentle proddings, to become gentlemen. We were beginning to grow up. And she was beginning to let go.

Mom consistently loved us passionately and yet held on to us loosely in love. The day Jeff and I turned sixteen she drove us to get our driver's licenses. Thirty minutes later she let us drive our old Volkswagen twelve hundred miles from Phoenix to Indianapolis to see our uncle. She wanted to go with us, but her hands and knees were too painful to sit scrunched in a small car for that long. Every time I look back, I marvel at the loose hold she had on our lives.

She held everything loosely. Cups. Silverware. Pencils. She even held the days loosely, never knowing whether it would be a good day or a bad one, taking what came and taking it with grace. If her gentle touch helped us grow up, it also provided a strong incentive to do what was right. Because her hands hurt so much, my mother was never able to spank us, but beneath her tender ways there was an underlying firmness. Worse than a spanking was when she would place her hand on ours, always gently, and speak to us, always gently, of her concern about our behavior. When she looked up at you and held your hand, you might as well have been in the grip of a lumberjack. You couldn't pull away. It would hurt her hands if you did. So you sat there. And you listened. And little by little, the warmth of her heart melted yours.

I have pictures in my mind of her typing, bending down to the keyboard, leaning a little to the right and typing at an angle. It's the way most people with rheumatoid arthritis have to type, if they can type at all. She would sit at the typewriter until the wee hours of the morning typing reports for us. I never thought much about those pictures then. Now I can't get them out of my mind. . .or my heart. . .

Four years after my dad left the hospice, my mom entered it. Her room was just three doors down from his. There she spent the last four months of her life.

This day I was pacing the hall outside that room, a bright orange form in my hand, trying to put off the inevitable.

We had talked about it a dozen times over the years and especially in the months leading up to this day. Yesterday I had gone over the whole thing again with Mom's primary care physician and the head nurse. And now I was the one who had to do it.

I was the one who had to walk into my mother's room, set that bright orange form in front of her, and have her sign it. It was the form reflecting her wish that there be no medical heroics in the last hours of her life.

It was the most difficult moment of my life.

Here sat my mother, my sweet, precious mother. Those bright piercing eyes. Her thinning snow-white hair. Her hands so warm and soft. We sat and held hands and talked. She was brave and courageous as ever.

I was a mess.

I cried at the thought of losing someone

who had loved me and blessed me since the day I was born. A thousand memories washed over me. Of walks and hugs, of breakfasts at the old kitchen table, and of camping trips in our beat-up old trailer. The days watching the Dodgers in spring training. The midnight runs for my can collection. Late-night crackers. I couldn't keep the tears from my eyes as I thought of losing her listening ear, her gentle love, her precious life.

It was the worst day of my life. How many more days would we have her? Two, three. A week?

Two weeks later, [my brother] Joe and I were keeping vigil in her room. I was sitting in the chair, taking the first shift. He was sleeping in the bed next to her. At 2:20 in the morning, her breathing grew shallow and irregular.

By now she had become so dehydrated she was unable to speak. But she didn't need to. She had said "I love you" hundreds of times with words and thousands of times with the pictures she left behind. No words needed to be spoken. No words needed to be heard.

As her breathing slowed, we moved our chairs next to her, one boy on each side, holding her hands. Hands that brushed away our tears and patted us gently when we had done well in sports or in school. Hands that put back so carefully the pieces of a broken heart. We nestled next to her just like when we were kids, when we got scared, or lonely, or just wanted to know that everything would be all right.

Only this time everything wouldn't be all right. This time she wouldn't be able to hug away the hurt.

Neither would we.

She breathed one last shallow breath. Neither Joe nor I moved. For several minutes we sat by her side, still and silent. Maybe if no one spoke, if no one stood up, if no one called the nurse, maybe we could somehow postpone the loss. Neither of us wanted to admit we had just lost our mother. . .and that we were now orphans.

I touched her hands for the last time. Those incredibly soft and tender hands.

I pray the first hands I see in heaven are the nail-scarred hands of my Savior.

And that the next ones I see are my mommy's.

Now straightened and strong.

But still soft and caring and lovely as I remembered them that day. . .and as I will remember them always.

THE WORD ON GENTLENESS

"Are there those among you who are truly wise and understanding? Then they should show it by living right and doing good things with a gentleness that comes from wisdom."

—James 3:13 NCV

"Let your gentleness be evident to all."

Philippians 4:5

"I, therefore, the prisoner of the Lord, beseech you to walk worthy of the calling with which you were called, with all lowliness and gentleness, with longsuffering, bearing with one another in love."

—Ephesians 4:1–2 NKJV

"A gentle answer turns away wrath, but a harsh word stirs up anger."

—Proverbs 15:1

"But in your hearts set apart Christ as Lord. Always be prepared to give an answer to everyone who asks you to give the reason for the hope that you have. But do this with gentleness and respect, keeping a clear conscience, so that those who speak maliciously against your good behavior in Christ may be ashamed of their slander."

—1 Peter 3:15–16

ॐ

THE WIND AND THE SUN
A Fable by Aesop

Once upon a time when everything could talk, the Wind and the Sun fell into an argument as to which was the stronger. Finally, they decided to put the matter to a test: they would see which one could make a certain man, who was walking along the road, throw off his cape.

The Wind tried first. He blew and he blew and he blew. The harder and colder he blew, the tighter the traveler wrapped his cape about him. The Wind finally gave up and told the Sun to try.

The Sun began to smile and as it grew warmer and warmer, the traveler was comfortable once more. But the Sun shone brighter and brighter until the man grew so hot, the sweat poured out on his face. He became weary, and seating himself on a stone, he quickly threw his cape to the ground.

You see, gentleness had accomplished what force could not.

୬

SPEAKING OF GENTLENESS. . .

"In our rough-and-rugged individualism, we think of gentleness as weakness, being soft, and virtually spineless. Not so!...Gentleness includes such enviable qualities as having strength under control, being calm and peaceful when surrounded by a heated atmosphere, emitting a soothing effect on those who may be angry or otherwise beside themselves, and possessing tact and gracious courtesy that causes others to retain their self-esteem and dignity. . . . Instead of losing, the gentle gain. Instead of being ripped off and taken advantage of, they come out ahead!"

—Charles R. Swindoll,
as quoted in *Draper's Book
of Quotations for the
Christian World*

"Although the world tells us to be assertive, the Word tells us to be gentle."

—Florence Littauer, in
The Best of Florence Littauer

"I've learned that a hug from my husband sends his strength into my body."

—39-year-old woman,
as quoted in *The Complete Live
and Learn and Pass It On*

*"Lord, make my words soft
and gentle today. . . .
I may have to eat them tomorrow!"*

Anonymous prayer

"Gentleness and consideration are qualities ascribed to Jesus himself, even though He is the all-powerful King. . . . Strikingly, [gentleness] is one of the traits required in spiritual leaders and is a mark of spiritual maturity and of responsiveness to God's Spirit. It is also the way set out in the New Testament for believers to respond to opposition."

—Lawrence O. Richards, in
Expository Dictionary of Bible Words

"Advice is like snow; the softer it falls, the longer it dwells upon and the deeper it sinks into the mind."

—Samuel Taylor Coleridge,
as quoted in *Christian Reader*,
Vol. 33, number 1

"It's easier to get close to someone when there are no hard edges."

—Roman the Teddy Bear,
as quoted in Susan E. Schwartz's
Teddy Bear Philosophy

"God strikes with his finger, and not with all his arm."

—George Herbert,
in *Jacula Prudentum*

"Gentleness is love's conduct."

—Paul Nadon,
in an Internet posting

"Many of us believe gentleness is something beyond our reach. Of course, that is simply not true. We can become gentle people, because God is gentle."

—James A. Chase,
in the Internet sermon,
"A Recipe for Right Relationships, Part 8"

No Match for Third Grade?

By all rights, Darlene Hanneman is no match for a classroom full of rowdy third-graders. Third-graders are loud and excitable. Darlene is quiet and calm. Third-graders are easily distracted by flashy events happening outside—like another class breaking early for recess. Darlene is focused and deliberate. Third-graders need a teacher with a foghorn-like voice to cut through the chatter with the day's homework assignments. Darlene speaks in a mild, pleasant tone, more like a hummingbird than a foghorn.

In short, the gentle woman should be hopelessly outgunned when faced with the task of teaching eight- and nine-year-olds important subjects like reading, writing, and arithmetic. And yet, she's one of the best.

Instead of yelling for kids to be quiet, she silences with a gaze or a gentle touch on a child's shoulder. Instead of being feared, she's respected. Instead of loudly cheering a child's accomplishment, she warms him or her with a sincere smile.

When our son entered Darlene's class, we wondered if Tony and his energetic classmates would soon overwhelm her. Then she came to visit Tony in our home. We noticed his immediate responsiveness to her gentle style. As she sat on our couch, she pleasantly invited him to sit next to her, giving him her full attention when he spoke and reassuring his contributions to the conversation with a light touch on the knee. She clearly explained her expectations regarding Tony's classroom conduct, but without resorting to the "fire-and-brimstone" style speech that usually accompanies such talk.

Later, we observed her deftly directing two dozen kids in a series of dramatic readings for parents. As we watched our son happily—and carefully—reading his part as "Toad" in a *Frog and Toad* story, we realized he was performing for her as much as he was for us. Her gentle and caring spirit had won him over, and it showed.

Yes, it might look like the soft-spoken and grandmotherly demeanor of Darlene Hanneman is no match for third-graders, but appearances can be deceiving. In fact, this wonderful teacher is the perfect match for this classroom, and we think parents can learn a lot from her as well.

A Prayer of Mary Batchelor[38]

Lord Jesus, give me your gentleness.

Make me sensitive to others' needs, quick to discern even when no words are spoken.

Help me never to rush in with thoughtless words, nor to brush others aside with sweeping assertions.

Help me never to quench another's hopes nor deepen another's sorrow, but to pour your peace and balm, your comfort and love on all those I meet today. Amen.

❧

In 1 Kings chapter 19, the Bible records a surprisingly gentle encounter Elijah the prophet had with God. We'd like to retell it for you here in our own words. . .

God in a Whisper

Elijah couldn't help but smile and feel proud of himself. He—well, God really—had just defeated hundreds of the false prophets Queen Jezebel had set up to lead the people of Israel in worshiping bloody idols of evil. The contest had been fantastic! In the end, God had swooped down with a blaze of fire and defeated once and for all the terrible power of Jezebel's false religion.

Or so it seemed.

As Elijah sat breathing the sweet breath of victory, he saw a messenger approaching. Moments later, the runner delivered this news: "King Ahab has told his wife Queen Jezebel about everything that happened today, and about how all her prophets have been killed. The Queen sends this message to you, Elijah: 'May the gods deal with me, be it ever so severely, if by this time tomorrow I do not make your life like that of one of them.'"

Sudden fear seized Elijah's heart. That madwoman was going to kill him! Elijah didn't waste any time. Immediately, he gathered his few things and ran for his life! He ran until he could run no more, and found himself a day's journey into the desert. There, he fell down under the branches of a broom tree and prayed.

"Where are you now, Lord? Have you gone away and taken your power with you? Why not end it right now, Lord? Why not kill me where I sit instead of making me wait for Jezebel's men to come and slit my throat? Oh, God, where have you gone and why did you leave me?"

Elijah collapsed in a heap under the tree and wept. Then he sat up with a start—something was poking him! Through slitted eyes Elijah was stunned to see an angel standing beside him, standing as if he'd been there all the time.

"Get up and eat," the angel said simply. And he produced bread and water. Elijah ate, drank, and lay back down. Not long after, the angel appeared again, this time saying "Get up and eat, for the journey is too much for you." Elijah obeyed.

Strengthened by this food from heaven, Elijah traveled forty days and nights across the desert until he reached Mount Horeb, the mountain of God. He slept that night in a cave at the base of the mountain.

Next morning, he heard the voice of God speaking to him. "What are you doing here, Elijah?"

The prophet replied, "I have been very zealous for the LORD God Almighty. The Israelites have rejected your covenant, broken down your altars, and put your prophets to death with the sword. I am the only one left, and now they are trying to kill me too."

God commanded, "Go out and stand on the mountain in the presence of the Lord, for the Lord is about to pass by."

Almost before Elijah could reach the entrance to the cave, he felt the wind—a rushing, mighty wind that tore through the landscape and left a waste of desolation behind it. Tree limbs cracked and broke in the face of the wind. Boulders rolled and shattered. Stinging dirt and dust blinded Elijah's eyes. But the Lord did not come.

Finally, the wind died down, and following closely on its heels Elijah felt the ground begin to tremble. In seconds a mighty earthquake cracked the ground, a yawning, terrible groan that surely announced the arrival of the Lord. . . But still, the Lord did not come.

After the earthquake came a monstrous fire that devoured everything it happened to touch. Elijah stood in fear, terrified he would soon be swallowed up in the flames of God. Almost as abruptly as it had come, the fire disappeared, leaving behind the sooty rubble of its destruction.

But still, in spite of the awesome power of the fire, the Lord had not come.

After the fire, silence filled the mountain. The world was still, nothing moving or turning. Elijah sat like a stone, unsure of whether or not he was even breathing.

Then he heard it. A gentle whisper caressed the battered ground, toying with his hearing in delightful tones. The whisper came again, and Elijah couldn't help but smile, sensing the Presence that accompanied the voice.

God had finally come, not in earthshaking power, but in the gentle, fragrant voice of a Friend.

❦

In his enchanting children's novel, The Lion, the Witch and the Wardrobe, *C. S. Lewis relates a beautiful example of gentleness bound in strength. In this scene, the great Lion, Aslan (a Christ-figure in the book), has just risen from the dead and greeted two of the children who love him, Susan and Lucy Pevensie, in front of the Stone Table where he had previously been executed. . .*

ASLAN'S ROMP[39]

"Oh, children," said the Lion, "I feel my strength coming back to me. Oh, children, catch me if you can!" He stood for a second, his eyes very bright, his limbs quivering, lashing himself with his tail.

Then he made a leap high over their heads and landed on the other side of the Table. Laughing, though she didn't know why, Lucy scrambled over it to reach him. Aslan leaped again. A mad chase began. Round and round the hill-top he led them, now hopelessly out of their reach, now letting them almost catch his tail, now diving between them, now tossing them in the air with his huge and beautifully velveted paws and catching them again, and now stopping unexpectedly so that all three of them rolled over together in a happy laughing heap of fur and arms and legs. It was such a romp as no one has ever had except in Narnia; and whether it was more like playing with a thunderstorm or playing with a kitten Lucy could never make up her mind. And the funny thing was that when all three finally lay together panting in the sun the girls no longer felt in the least tired or hungry or thirsty.

A Closing Prayer[40]

Lord of the gentle hands, may mine be gentle too.

9

The Fruit of the Spirit Is. . .

Self-Control

Wouldn't it be great if Adam and Eve had never given in to temptation? If they'd resisted the desire to taste the forbidden fruit in the Garden of Eden? If they'd exhibited enough self-control to save us all from that original sin?

But, sadly, they did give in to the serpent's tempting, and humanity has been paying the price ever since. Perhaps it's time we learn from their failure, and ask God to help us practice self-control, to resist temptation, and to let our lives glorify Him. As we understand it, it's never too late to start obeying God.

SMALL START, BIG FINISH

It all started with a cotton ball. That's it, really.

Well, there were also two doctors involved. Dr. Mohan Korgaonkar was the surgeon, and Dr. Kwok Wei Chan was assisting as the anesthesiologist. The patient shall remain nameless.

So there they were, Dr. Korgaonkar, Dr. Chan, our long-suffering patient (sleeping, thank goodness), and the cotton ball.

The date was October 24, 1991, and all was going as planned. An operation was scheduled and underway in a Worcester, Massachusetts, hospital. Dutifully doing his job, Dr. Chan administered the anesthesia, sending our patient into a deep slumber. With a confidence that comes from years of experience, Dr. Korgaonkar deftly began the procedure. All was going well.

Except, it seems, for our two physicians. No one knows for sure what words passed between them, but the intent was clear. These men didn't like each other.

Silently the minutes ticked by, and with each passing moment the tension in the operating room grew thicker. And thicker.

Perhaps Dr. Chan was a "backseat surgeon," offering unwanted advice about the surgeon's technique. Perhaps Dr. Korgaonkar told a belittling joke about anesthesiologists in general, or about Dr. Chan in particular. Perhaps one was having a bad hair day and the other noticed. Or, most likely, perhaps the two physicians were feeling a bit cranky, stressed, and tired.

Whatever the reason, at one point during the operation, something about Dr. Chan irked the surgeon. Almost without thinking, Dr. Korgaonkar flicked a cotton ball disdainfully at the anesthesiologist. Apparently, the surgeon was a good aim, because Dr. Chan retaliated.

Next came pushing and shouting. Then an all-out brawl between the two men of medicine. Fists flying and medical goals forgotten, the doctors eventually escalated into a wrestling-punching-jabbing-name-calling bout on the operating room floor. Both doctors had completely lost any semblance of self-control, their only aim to satisfy their rage.

And our patient? Slept through it all.

Finally the two men tired a bit, regained their composure, got up, and finished the operation. Not long after, both were fined $10,000 by the state Board of Registration in Medicine, and ordered to submit to joint psychotherapy for their aggressive tendencies.

And to think, it all started with a cotton ball.[41]

It only took a little cotton ball to send two respected doctors over the edge and into fisticuffs. And for their little indulgence, they succeeded in cheapening their reputation and the reputation of doctors in general. Truly, the $10,000 fine was the smallest fee they paid!

We would be wise to take a lesson from these poor examples of self-control. Hey, if a teeny little cotton ball can tear up a whole operating room, there's no telling what might happen if we don't!

ॐ

A DESERT PARABLE[42]

The story goes something like this:

Two travelers embarked on a dangerous journey across the desert. At first, all seemed to be going well. There was plenty of water, and the company was pleasant. But midway through the journey, one traveler noticed the terrain had suddenly become a vast, unrecognizable plain. Slowly their water supplies dwindled. They continued on, fear beginning to gnaw at their hearts. Finally, their fear became a reality.

They were lost and alone in the merciless, fiery desert.

Throats drying, lips parching, and now with water scarce, they wandered on hoping to find a way out. One day passed, then two. Finally, on the fifth day, when they were weak and dying of thirst, a miracle appeared. A stranger came into view, a man with camels and life-giving water!

The two travelers collapsed in a heap and prayed the stranger would see them—and he did. Moments later he stood before them, taking in the situation.

"Help me! Help me!" croaked the first traveler. "Need water! Must have water! Give me water! Water!"

The second traveler said nothing.

The first traveler began clawing at the stranger, all the while pleading and begging for water. Still, the second man said nothing, waiting. Intrigued, the stranger broke free from the first traveler and knelt down beside the second.

"Are you thirsty?" the stranger inquired.

"Yes. Very," he replied.

"Then why do you not cry out for water like your friend here?"

"The water belongs to you," said the second

traveler. "If you choose to share it, I won't have to ask."

Impressed by this traveler's self-restraint even in harsh circumstances, the stranger unstoppered his flask and poured the life-giving liquid down the thirsty man's throat. Only after the second traveler had drunk his fill did the first get his share.

Self-control had won what wailing demands had not.

❧

DISCIPLINE YOURSELF (NO ONE ELSE WILL)
by Bruce & Stan

Humans are funny beings. It used to be that many of us wanted every material thing we could get our hands on, and we wanted whatever it was to be bigger, better, or faster. Then we discovered that *outward* material things don't make us happy. So over the last few years we've turned *inward*. We've decided that it's what's inside that counts. Consequently, many of us have embarked on an inward journey, seeking to simplify our lifestyles while increasing our joy.

At least that's the goal, because that's what the simplicity gurus are telling us in books like *Simple Abundance* and *Living the Simple Life*.

The idea of simplifying your life is a good one. . . . The problem is that we are attacking the goal with the same unbridled zest we used to collect all that stuff in the first place. Like a crazy pendulum, we swing from one extreme to the other with gusto, somehow feeling empty at both places.

So how do you find the satisfaction you've been looking for? The key is balance, consistency, and perseverance, all of which come from one thing and one thing only: *discipline*.

Here's our dilemma. We want it all, and we want it now, whether it's an abundance of possessions or an abundance of simplicity. But nothing worthwhile comes quickly, and nothing worthwhile comes without discipline. Over life's long haul, discipline works in every dimension of your life: financial, physical, mental, and spiritual. If you've ever tried to get rich quick, tried to lose weight by taking a pill, tried to get knowledge by cramming at the last minute, or attempted to get close to God by asking for a miracle, you know what we're talking about.

It's easy to get caught in the trap of quick

results when you focus on the results rather than the journey. The truth is, the joy is in the journey, in the daily discipline of growing in the details of your mind, body, and spirit. The only way to bring abundance to your life—the kind of abundance that gives you joy—is to bring discipline into your life. . .

- Discipline begins with small things done daily.
- The secret behind most success stories? Discipline.
- Every morning you choose your attitude for the day.
- The first step on the path to commitment is making up your mind.
- You can plan to succeed or you can plan to fail. The choice is yours.
- Motivation increases when we assume large responsibilities with a short deadline.
- Develop a cause for your life. Whatever it is, dedicate yourself to it daily.
- Don't be good at making excuses.
- Discipline is at the heart of discipleship.
- Before diving into anything, step back and view the big picture.

- Acquire good habits; abandon bad habits.
- Move from involvement to commitment.
- Use your free time productively.
- Your dreams won't come true if you allow them to languish.
- Your dreams won't come true if you're sleeping.
- If you want to achieve excellence, begin with discipline.
- Worthwhile activities may be tough in the short-term but rewarding in the long-term.
- People will be more impressed by what you finish than by what you start.
- Motivation can fade. Habits prevail.

Unfortunately, American society isn't known for its self-control, and so we often reap the dismal rewards of our own bad habits. . .

AMERICA'S BAD HABITS[43]

There are approximately sixty-one million cigarette smokers in the United States today, or roughly 29 percent of the U.S. population aged twelve and older. Those smokers incur a cost of an estimated $60 billion a year in smoking-related health care (not counting lost productivity for missing work on account of a smoking-related illness). Also, an estimated 400,000 deaths per year are attributed to smoking cigarettes.

Smokers tend to drink twice as much alcohol as non-smokers, and a smoker's risk of drinking too heavily is ten to fourteen times higher than that of a non-smoker. Additionally, smokers are over four times more likely to abuse illicit drugs than non-smokers.

Americans spend over $100 billion each year on alcohol consumption. Alcohol is involved in 44 percent of the nation's annual traffic-accident fatalities, a number that's roughly equal to 17,600 people each year. One of alcohol's many negative side effects, liver cirrhosis, is the eleventh leading cause of death among Americans. Additionally, roughly one out of every three deaths by drowning is alcohol-related.

With nearly sixty-nine million Americans over age twelve using it, marijuana is the most frequently used illegal drug in the U.S.A. Marijuana hinders a person's short-term memory, warps perceptions, and slows reaction time. With that in mind, it's no surprise to discover that one study revealed that roughly one-third of hospital trauma patients are admitted due to marijuana-related accidents. Additionally, the likelihood of using cocaine has been estimated to be more than 104 times greater for those who have tried marijuana than for those who have never tried it.

Roughly twenty-two million Americans have used cocaine, one of the most addictive drugs of abuse. One out of every ten people who begin using cocaine "recreationally" will go on to serious, heavy abuse of this drug. As recently as 1995, the number of cocaine-related hospital emergencies during a given year was over 140,000 incidents, or roughly one-fourth of all drug-related emergency room treatments.

We could go on, but we're betting you get the picture. Individual Americans' inability to exercise self-control has resulted in deadly habits for America as a whole. Are you part of these statistics? Perhaps you can change them for the better, starting right now.

THE FLIES AND THE HONEY POT[44]
by Aesop

A jar of honey chanced to spill
Its contents on the windowsill
In many a viscous pool and rill.

The flies, attracted by the sweet,
Began so greedily to eat,
They smeared their fragile wings and feet.

With many a twitch and pull in vain
They gasped to get away again,
And died in aromatic pain.

Moral:
O foolish creatures that destroy
Themselves for transitory joy.

A LESSON ON GOSSIP FROM WINSTON CHURCHILL[45]

We're told this story is true, and believe it to be so. But whether it is fact or make-believe, the point it makes about controlling our speech remains the same.

In the days after World War II, English Prime Minister Winston Churchill was found attending an official ceremony in London. Sitting behind him were two men who recognized the statesman. Shaking their heads in disdain, they began whispering between themselves about the politician in front of them.

"They say Churchill's quite senile now," whispered one.

"Yes, they say he's doing England more harm than good," the other whispered back.

"They say he should step aside and leave the running of this government to younger, more dynamic people," continued the first man.

Then, quite abruptly, their malicious gossip ceased when old Churchill turned around and roared, "They also say he's quite deaf!"

One of the founding fathers of our country, Ben Franklin, had much to share on the topic of self-control. Listen to a smattering of his wise advice gathered here for you.

BEN FRANKLIN ON SELF-CONTROL[46]

- If you would be wealthy, think of saving more than getting.
- If you know how to spend less than you get, you have the philosopher's stone.
- Sell not virtue to purchase wealth, nor liberty to purchase power.
- Spare and have is better than spend and crave.
- He that lieth down with dogs shall rise up with fleas.
- Keep your eyes wide open before marriage, half shut afterwards.
- 'Tis easier to suppress the first desire than to satisfy all that follow it.
- He is a governor that governs his passions, and he is a servant that serves them.
- Eat few suppers and you'll need few medicines.

- Eat to live, live not to eat.
- Life with fools consists in drinking; with the wise man, living's thinking.
- The excellency of hogs is fatness; of men, virtue.
- Little strokes, fell great oaks.
- God gives all things to industry.
- Dost thou love life? Then do not squander time; for that's the stuff life is made of.
- The honest man takes pains, and then enjoys pleasures; the knave takes pleasure, and then suffers pains.
- Work as if you were to live 100 years, pray as if you were to die tomorrow.

❧

THE WORD ON SELF-CONTROL

"So then, let us not be like others, who are asleep, but let us be alert and self-controlled. For those who sleep, sleep at night, and those who get drunk, get drunk at night. But since we belong to the day, let us be self-controlled, putting on faith and love as a breastplate, and the hope of salvation as a helmet."

—1 Thessalonians 5:6–8

"We all make many mistakes, but those who control their tongues can also control themselves in every other way. We can make a large horse turn around and go wherever we want by means of a small bit in its mouth. And a tiny rudder makes a huge ship turn wherever the pilot wants it to go, even though the winds are strong. So also, the tongue is a small thing, but what enormous damage it can do."

—James 3:2–5 NLT

"Like a city whose walls are
broken down is a man
who lacks self-control."
Proverbs 25:28

"All athletes practice strict self-control. They do it to win a prize that will fade away, but we do it for an eternal prize. So I run straight to the goal with purpose in every step. I am not like a boxer who misses his punches. I discipline my body like an athlete, training it to do what it should. Otherwise, I fear that after preaching to others I myself might be disqualified."

—1 Corinthians 9:25–27 NLT

"So prepare your minds for service and have self-control. All your hope should be for the gift of grace that will be yours when Jesus Christ is shown to you."

—1 Peter 1:13 NCV

❧

DISCIPLINE OF THE HEART
by Amy Nappa and Jody Brolsma

On her wedding day, Shari Hayes was a size 20. Her new husband loved her, and friends who had gathered on this special day declared she looked radiant. But Shari felt differently inside.

"I didn't like myself," she shares. "I knew God loved me no matter what, but He wanted to work in my life and make me grow."

So shortly after her wedding day and with the support of her husband, Dan, Shari began one of the ultimate tests of self-control. A diet.

Yes, we've all been on diets. Some with success, most without. Shari had tried other diets too, but this time she was determined to succeed. So instead of starving herself with celery sticks and grapefruit juice, or counting every calorie, Shari made big changes in her life.

First, of course, was eating. "I had to change my eating habits and learn how to eat right." Next, she disciplined herself in exercise. "Exercise can be hard," she admits, "I tried to exercise with a friend for accountability, fun, and encouragement." She sought encouragement from the Scriptures by hanging verses about her home to help her say "no" to temptation. And her loving husband added incentive by offering her a dollar for every pound lost. "We didn't have a lot of money, but a little helped."

Sounds so simple, but we all know from experience that it wasn't. The self-control required for dieting is long-term, not just turning down dessert once a week. Shari remembers, "The hardest part was that it took a long time. One and a half years, slow and steady. It was a long haul but it paid off." Of course Shari got discouraged at times, but instead of indulging in chocolate cake, she treated herself to a new scarf or a video. And the compliments of friends who noticed her slimmer body did wonders to keep her on course as well.

As a result of the discipline of those long months Shari lost eighty pounds. She went from a size 20 to a size 8. Dan gave her the $80 and she went out to spend it all on new, smaller, clothes. And, even more amazingly, Snari has kept that weight off for more than ten years. This truly was a permanent change of lifestyle for her.

Is thinness a virtue? No. However, discipline and self-control are, and Shari certainly has demonstrated these in her life. She doesn't hide away her wedding pictures. Instead, she's proud to tell others of how God helped her reach a difficult goal. She is teaching her daughters a healthful lifestyle and, most importantly, is teaching them to follow God.

Shari encourages us in her own words:

"Seek the Lord when you know God wants you to do something. I wanted to please Him most of all. My motivation was to make the Lord proud and ask for His strength in my weakness. He wants to give us victory through anything that is pleasing to Him. Don't give up. Keep going toward your goal even if you feel it's too far away."

Loving God, You have the strength to move mountains. Give us the strength to move away from the refrigerator.

DIETRICH BONHOEFFER ON TEMPTATION[47]

In our members there is a slumbering inclination towards desire which is both sudden and fierce. With irresistible power, desire seizes mastery over the flesh. All at once a secret, smoldering fire is kindled. The flesh burns and is in flames. It makes no difference whether it is sexual desire or ambition or vanity or desire for revenge or love of fame and power or greed for money or, finally, that strange desire for the beauty of the world, of nature. Joy in God is. . . extinguished in us and we seek all our joy in the creature. At this moment God is quite unreal to us, He loses all reality, and only desire for the creature is real; the only reality is the devil. Satan does not fill us with hatred of God, but with forgetfulness of God. . . . The lust thus aroused envelopes the mind and will of man in deepest darkness. The powers of clear discrimination and of decision are taken from us.

Adam and Eve's failure to exercise self-control at the dawn of creation had devastating consequences. It's a grim memory, but one by which we can be reminded of the benefits of resisting temptation.

BETRAYAL IN THE GARDEN
(GENESIS 3)

Now the serpent was more crafty than any of the wild animals the LORD God had made. He said to the woman, "Did God really say, 'You must not eat from any tree in the garden'?"

The woman said to the serpent, "We may eat fruit from the trees in the garden, but God did say, 'You must not eat fruit from the tree that is in the middle of the garden, and you must not touch it, or you will die.'"

"You will not surely die," the serpent said to the woman. "For God knows that when you eat of it your eyes will be opened, and you will be like God, knowing good and evil."

When the woman saw that the fruit of the tree was good for food and pleasing to the eye, and also desirable for gaining wisdom, she took some and ate it. She also gave some to her husband, who was with her, and he ate it. Then the eyes of both of them were opened, and they realized they were naked; so they sewed fig leaves together and made coverings for themselves.

Then the man and his wife heard the sound of the LORD God as he was walking in the garden in the cool of the day, and they hid from the LORD God among the trees of the garden. But the LORD God called to the man, "Where are you?"

He answered, "I heard you in the garden, and I was afraid because I was naked; so I hid."

And he said, "Who told you that you were naked? Have you eaten from the tree that I commanded you not to eat from?"

The man said, "The woman you put here with me—she gave me some fruit from the tree, and I ate it."

Then the LORD God said to the woman, "What is this you have done?"

The woman said, "The serpent deceived me, and I ate."

So the LORD God said to the serpent, "Because you have done this,

"Cursed are you above all the livestock
and all the wild animals!
You will crawl on your belly
and you will eat dust

all the days of your life.
And I will put enmity
between you and the woman,
and between your offspring and hers;
he will crush your head,
and you will strike his heel."

To the woman he said,
    "I will greatly increase your pains
in childbearing; with pain you will
give birth to children.
Your desire will be for your husband,
and he will rule over you."

To Adam he said,
    "Because you listened to your wife
and ate from the tree about which I
commanded you, 'You must not eat of it,'
"Cursed is the ground because of you;
through painful toil you will eat of it
all the days of your life.
It will produce thorns and thistles for you,
and you will eat the plants of the field.
By the sweat of your brow
you will eat your food
until you return to the ground,
since from it you were taken;

for dust you are
and to dust you will return."

Adam named his wife Eve, because she would become the mother of all the living.

The Lord God made garments of skin for Adam and his wife and clothed them. And the Lord God said, "The man has now become like one of us, knowing good and evil. He must not be allowed to reach out his hand and take also from the tree of life and eat, and live forever." So the Lord God banished him from the Garden of Eden to work the ground from which he had been taken. After he drove the man out, he placed on the east side of the Garden of Eden cherubim and a flaming sword flashing back and forth to guard the way to the tree of life.

ॐ

A Prayer of Self-Control from William Barclay[48]

O God,
    Control my tongue.
    Keep me from saying things which make trouble, and from involving myself in arguments

which only make bad situations worse and which get nowhere. Control my thoughts.

Shut the door of my mind against all envious and jealous thoughts; shut it against all bitter and resentful thoughts; shut it against all ugly and unclean thoughts.

Help me live today in purity, in humility, and in love.

Through Jesus Christ my Lord. Amen.

ABOUT THE AUTHORS

Mike & Amy Nappa are founders of the Christian media organization, Nappaland Communications, Inc. They are best-selling authors with over a half-million copies of their books in print, and have been featured in national TV, radio, and print media. They both serve as contributing editors for *CBA Frontline* magazine, and write monthly columns for *Parent Life* and *Living with Teenagers* magazines. Additionally, their writing has appeared in many other fine publications such as *CCM*, *Children's Ministry*, *Christian Parenting Today*, *Christian Single*, *Family Fun*, *Focus on the Family Clubhouse* and *Clubhouse Jr.*, *Group*, *Home Life*, *New Man*, *Profile*, *Release*, and more. The Nappas make their home in Colorado where they're active in their church. To contact Mike and Amy, send e-mail to Nappaland@aol.com.

CREDITS

NOTES

THE FRUIT OF THE SPIRIT IS. . .
LOVE

1. As quoted in *The Christian's Treasury* edited and compiled by Lissa Roche. (Crossway Books, 1995).

2. As told in *Humor for Preaching and Teaching*, edited by Edward K. Rowell. (Baker Book House, 1996).

THE FRUIT OF THE SPIRIT IS. . .
JOY

3. As quoted in *Eerdmans' Book of Famous Prayers*, compiled by Veronica Zundel. (Grand Rapids, Mich.: William B. Eerdmans Publishing Company, 1983), 51.

4. *1001 Great Stories and Quotes* by R. Kent Hughes. (Wheaton, Ill.: Tyndale House Publishers, 1998), 304.

5. As quoted in *Ask Me If I Care* by Nancy Rubin. (Berkeley, Calif.: Ten Speed Press, 1994), 147.

6. *Worship and Service Hymnal.* (Chicago, Ill.: Hope Publishing Company, 1957), hymn number 365.

7. Source for language translations is *Travlang's Translating Dictionary*, http://dictionaries.travlang.com/

8. As quoted in *Conversations with God*, edited by James Melvin Washington, Ph.D. (New York: Harper Collins Publishers, 1994), 190.

9. *America in Search of Its Soul* by Gibson Winter. (Harrisburg, Pa.: Morehouse Publishing, 1996), 2–3.

10. As quoted in *Eerdmans' Book of Famous Prayers*, compiled by Veronica Zundel. (Grand Rapids, Mich.: William B. Eerdmans Publishing Company, 1983), 30.

THE FRUIT OF THE SPIRIT IS. . . PATIENCE

11. As quoted in *The Doubleday Prayer Collection*, selected and arranged by Mary Batchelor. (New York: Doubleday, 1992 & 1996), 412.

12. *It Takes Endurance* by Eugene Robinson. (Sisters, Ore.: Multnomah Publishers, 1998), 16–17.

13. As quoted in *The Communion of Saints*, edited by Horton Davies. (Grand Rapids, Mich.: William B. Eerdmans Publishing Company, 1990), 94.

14. From *Expository Dictionary of Bible Words*, (Grand Rapids, Mich.: Regency Reference Library, 1985), 478.

15. "Why We Pray," *Life* (March 1994): 58.

16. *In the Trenches* by Reggie White. (Nashville, Tenn.: Thomas Nelson Publishers, 1996), 173–85.

THE FRUIT OF THE SPIRIT IS. . . KINDNESS

17. As quoted by Frederick Buechner in "What are We Going to Be?" *Preaching Today*, Tape 56.

18. As quoted in *The Book of Virtues,* edited, with commentary, by William J. Bennett. (New York: Simon & Schuster, 1993), 147.

19. As quoted in *The Communion of the Saints*, edited by Horton Davies. (Grand Rapids, Mich.: William B. Eerdmans Publishing Company, 1990).

20. "The Big Picture: Staying Afloat" by Charles Hirshberg. *Life* (August 1996): 8.

21. As quoted in *Illustrations Unlimited* (Wheaton, Ill.: Tyndale House Publishers, Inc, 1988), 119.

22. As quoted in *Letters Home* by George Grant and Karen Grant. (Nashville, Tenn.: Cumberland House, 1997), 82–83.

THE FRUIT OF THE SPIRIT IS. . . GOODNESS

23. From *The Day America Told the Truth*, by James Patterson and Peter Kim. (New York: Prentice Hall Press, 1991), 119–27.

24. "Tiny Archibald, Basketball Hall of Famer" by John O'Keefe. *Sports Illustrated* (November 9, 1998): 22.

25. "Personal Glimpses: Encouraging Words" by Stephen Rubello. *Reader's Digest* (February 1996): 125–26.

26. *The Knowledge of the Holy* by A.W. Tozer. (San Francisco, Calif.: Harper & Row Publishers, 1961).

27. As quoted in *A Treasury of Wisdom*,
compiled by Ken and Angela Abraham.
(Uhrichsville, Ohio: Barbour Publishing,
1996), July 4 page.

28. Zondervan Publishing House e-mail Alert
Service, M|Wire, June 25 and September
17, 1998.

29. Zondervan Publishing House e-mail Alert
Service, *The Pastor's File*, April 1998.

30. Zondervan News Service, September 1998.

31. A note to the reader: We originally discovered this story in the encouraging book *And
the Angels Were Silent* by Max Lucado.

However, when we contacted the publisher
of that book, they informed us that Max
Lucado had obtained the details of the
story and the quotes of John Blanchard
from an unknown source. If you know,
and can verify, the original source, please
contact Barbour Publishing so we can

properly credit this story in future editions of this book.

32. As quoted in *Letters Home* by George Grant and Karen Grant. (Nashville, Tenn.: Cumberland House, 1997), 165–66.

33. *America's Dumbest Dates*, by Merry Block Jones. (Andrews McMeel Publishing, 1998), 63.

34. "Love Endures as Memory Goes," *The Arizona Republic* (September 29, 1998): D1–D2.

35. "Workin' 5 to 9" by Edward K. Rowell. *Leadership* (April 15, 1998).

36. Phone interview with Max Lucado, conducted by Mike Nappa on September 3, 1998.

37. As quoted in *Thoughts for the Journey 1999 Calendar* (Wheaton, Ill.: Tyndale House Publishers, 1998), January 9, 1999 page.

THE FRUIT OF THE SPIRIT IS. . .
GENTLENESS

38. *The Doubleday Prayer Collection*, selected and arranged by Mary Batchelor. (New York: Doubleday, 1992 & 1996), 421.

39. Quoted from *The Lion, the Witch and the Wardrobe* by C. S. Lewis. (New York: Collier Books, 1950), 160–61.

40. As quoted in *The Doubleday Prayer Collection*, selected and arranged by Mary Batchelor. (New York: Doubleday, 1992 & 1996), 421.

THE FRUIT OF THE SPIRIT IS. . .
SELF-CONTROL

41. "Doctors fined for brawl during operation." *The Coloradoan* (Sunday, November 28, 1993): A3.

42. *Sinbad's Guide to Life* by Sinbad with David Ritz. (New York: Bantam Books, 1997), 81–82.

43. Statistics taken from: "Closing in on Addiction" by Kristin Leutwyler and Alan Hall. *Scientific American* web site, November 24, 1997; "What If. . ." by various authors. *American Demographics* (December 1997): 39–45; and *The National Clearinghouse for Alcohol and Drug Information* web site.

44. As quoted in *The Book of Virtues*, edited and with commentary by William J. Bennett. (New York: Simon and Schuster, 1993), 48.

45. *Humor for Preaching and Teaching* edited by Ed Rowell. (Grand Rapids, Mich.: Baker Books, 1996), 48.

46. As quoted in *The Moral of the Story* compiled and edited by Jerry Newcombe. (Nashville, Tenn.: Broadman & Holman Publishers, 1996), 145–46, 249, 258–59, 288–89.

47. As quoted in *The Tale of the Tardy Oxcart* by Charles R. Swindoll. (Nashville, Tenn.: Word Publishing, 1998), 566.

48. As quoted in *The Doubleday Prayer Collection*, selected and arranged by Mary Batchelor. (New York: Doubleday, 1992 & 1996), 425.

Inspirational Library

Beautiful purse/pocket-size editions of Christian classics bound in flexible leatherette. These books make thoughtful gifts for everyone on your list, including yourself!

When I'm on My Knees The highly popular collection of devotional thoughts on prayer, especially for women.
  Flexible Leatherette $4.97

The Bible Promise Book Over 1,000 promises from God's Word arranged by topic. What does God promise about matters like: Anger, Illness, Jealousy, Love, Money, Old Age, and Mercy? Find out in this book!
  Flexible Leatherette $3.97

Daily Wisdom for Women A daily devotional for women seeking biblical wisdom to apply to their lives. Scripture taken from the New American Standard Version of the Bible.
  Flexible Leatherette $4.97

My Daily Prayer Journal Each page is dated and features a Scripture verse and ample room for you to record your thoughts, prayers, and praises. One page for each day of the year.
  Flexible Leatherette $4.97

Available wherever books are sold.
Or order from:

Barbour Publishing, Inc.
P.O. Box 719
Uhrichsville, OH 44683
http://www.barbourbooks.com

If you order by mail add $2.00 to your order for shipping.
Prices subject to change without notice.

Reaganomics

Conservatism - lie of
indiv enterprise. If only
tax breaks to capitalists,
will revive economy. This is
long gone myth

Writes about Hoover + Roosevelt

JOHN DEWEY

Individualism
Old and New

CAPRICORN BOOKS
G. P. PUTNAM'S SONS
NEW YORK

PREFATORY NOTE

I AM OBLIGED to the courtesy of the editors of *The New Republic* for permission to use material that originally appeared in the columns of that journal and which is now incorporated in connection with considerable new matter, in this volume. It is a pleasure to acknowledge my particular indebtedness to Mr. Daniel Mebane, the treasurer of *The New Republic,* for valuable suggestions and assistance.

CONTENTS

INDIVIDUALISM
OLD AND NEW

INDIVIDUALISM
OLD AND NEW

CHAPTER I

THE HOUSE DIVIDED AGAINST ITSELF

IT IS BECOMING a commonplace to say that in thought and feeling, or at least in the language in which they are expressed, we are living in some bygone century, anywhere from the thirteenth to the eighteenth, although physically and externally we belong to the twentieth century. In such a contradictory condition, it is not surprising that a report of American life, such as is contained, for example, in "Middletown," should frequently refer to a "bewildered" or "confused" state of mind as characteristic of us.

Anthropologically speaking, we are living in a money culture. Its cult and rites dominate. "The money medium of exchange and the cluster of activities associated with its acquisition drastically condition the other activities of the people." This, of course, is as it should be; people have to make a living, do they not? And for what should they work if not for money, and how should they get goods and enjoyments if not by buying them with money—thus enabling someone else to make more money, and in the end to start shops and factories to give employment to still others, so that they can make more money to enable other people to make more money by selling goods—and so on indefinitely. So far, all is for the best in the best of all possible cultures: our rugged—or is it ragged?—individualism.

And if the culture pattern works out so that society is divided into two classes, the working group and the business (including professional) group, with two and a half times as many in the former as in the latter, and with the chief ambition of parents in the former class that their children should climb into the latter, that is doubtless because American life offers such unparalleled opportunities for each individual to prosper according to his virtues. If few workers know what they are making or the meaning of what they do, and still fewer know what becomes of the work of their hands—in the largest industry of Middletown perhaps one-tenth of one per cent of the product is consumed locally—this is doubtless because we have so perfected our system of distribution that the whole country is one. And if the mass of workers live in constant fear of loss of their jobs, this is doubtless because our spirit of progress, manifest in change of fashions, invention of new machines and power of over-production, keeps everything on the move. Our reward of industry and thrift is so accurately adjusted to individual ability that it is natural and proper that the workers should look forward with dread to the age of fifty or fifty-five, when they will be laid on the shelf.

All this we take for granted; it is treated as an inevitable part of our social system. To dwell on the dark side of it is to blaspheme against our religion of prosperity. But it is a system that calls for a hard and strenuous philosophy. If one looks at what we do and what happens, and then expects to find a theory of life that harmonizes with the actual situation, he will be shocked by the contradiction he comes upon. For the situation calls for assertion of complete economic determinism. We live as if economic forces determined the growth and decay of institutions and settled the fate of individuals. Liberty becomes a well-nigh obsolete term; we start, go, and stop at the signal of a vast industrial machine. Again, the actual system would seem to imply a pretty definitely materialistic scheme of value. Worth is measured by ability to hold one's own or to get ahead in a competitive pecuniary race. "Within the privacy of shabby or ambitious houses, marriage, birth, child-rearing, death, and the personal immensities of family life go forward. However, it is not so much these functional urgencies of life that determine how favorable this physical necessity shall be, but the extraneous detail of how much money the father earns." The philosophy appropriate to such a situation is that of struggle for existence and survival of the economically fit. One would expect the current theory of life, if it reflects the actual situation, to be the most drastic Darwinism. And, finally, one would anticipate that the personal traits most prized would be clear-sighted vision of personal advantage and resolute ambition to secure it at any human cost. Sentiment and sympathy would be at the lowest discount.

It is unnecessary to say that the current view of life in Middletown, in Anytown, is nothing of this sort. Nothing gives us Americans the horrors more than to hear that some misguided creature in some low part of the earth preaches what we practice—and practice much more efficiently than anyone else—namely, economic determinism. Our whole theory is that man plans and uses machines for his own humane and moral purposes, instead of being borne wherever the machine carries him. Instead of materialism, our idealism is probably the loudest and most frequently professed philosophy the world has ever heard. We praise even our most successful men, not for their ruthless and self-centered energy in getting ahead, but because of their love of flowers, children, and dogs, or their kindness to aged relatives. Anyone who frankly urges a selfish creed of life is everywhere frowned upon. Along with the disappearance of the home, and the multiplication of divorce in one generation by six hundred per cent, there is the most abun-

INDIVIDUALISM—OLD AND NEW

dant and most sentimental glorification of the sacredness of home and the beauties of constant love that history can record. We are surcharged with altruism and bursting with desire to "serve" others.

These are only a few of the obvious contradictions between our institutions and practice on one hand, and our creeds and theories on the other, contradictions which a survey of any of our Middletowns reveals. It is not surprising that the inhabitants of these towns are bewildered, uneasy, restless, always seeking something new and different, only to find, as a rule, the same old thing in a new dress. It may all be summed up, perhaps, by saying that nowhere in the world at any time has religion been so thoroughly respectable as with us, and so nearly totally disconnected from life. I hesitate to dwell on the revelation that this book gives of "religious" life in Middletown. The glorification of religion as setting the final seal of approval on pecuniary success, and supplying the active motive to more energetic struggle for such success, and the adoption by the churches of the latest devices of the movies and the advertiser, approach too close to the ob-

14

scene. Schooling is developed to the point where more pupils reach the high school than in other lands; and one-half of the pupils in the last years of the high school think that the first chapters of the Hebrew Scriptures give a more accurate account of the origin and early history of man than does science, and only one-fifth actively dissent. If the investigation had been made when a contain questionnaire was distributed among our school children, it is likely that the usual percentage of youth would have recorded their belief that Harding was the greatest man in the world. In another way, the whole story is told in brief when one contrasts what is actually happening to family life and the complete secularization of daily activities with a statement from the pulpit that "the three notable words in the English language are mother, home and heaven," a remark that would certainly pass unquestioned in any representative American audience.

It makes little difference whether one selects important or trivial aspects of the contradiction between our life as we outwardly live it and our thoughts and feelings—or what we at least say are our beliefs and sentiments. The significant question is: What is the cause of this split and contradiction? There are those, of course, who attribute it to the fact that people being, generally speaking, morons and boobs, they must be expected to act out the parts to which they are assigned. The "explanation" does not take us very far, even if one accepts it. The particular forms that the alleged boobery takes are left quite unaccounted for. And the more one knows of history, the more one comes to believe that traditions and institutions count more than native capacity or incapacity in explaining things. It is evident enough that the rapid industrialization of our civilization took us unawares. Being mentally and morally unprepared, our older creeds have become ingrowing; the more we depart from them in fact, the more loudly we proclaim them. In effect we treat them as magic formulæ. By repeating them often enough we hope to ward off the evils of the new situation, or at least to prevent ourselves from seeing them —and this latter function is ably performed by our nominal beliefs.

With an enormous command of instrumentalities, with possession of a secure technology, we glorify the past, and legalize and idealize the *status quo,* instead of seriously asking how we are to employ the means at our disposal so as to form an equitable and stable society. This is our great abdication. It explains how and why we are a house divided against itself. Our tradition, our heritage, is itself double. It contains in itself the ideal of equality of opportunity and of freedom for all, without regard to birth and status, as a condition for the effective realization of that equality. This ideal and endeavor in its behalf once constituted our essential Americanism; that which was prized as the note of a new world. It is the genuinely spiritual element of our tradition. No one can truthfully say that it has entirely disappeared. But its promise of a new moral and religious outlook has not been attained. It has not become the well-spring of a new intellectual consensus; it is not (even unconsciously) the vital source of any distinctive and shared philosophy. It directs our politics only spasmodically, and while it has generously provided schools it does not control their aims or their methods.

17

Meanwhile our institutions embody another and older tradition. Industry and business conducted for money profit are nothing new; they are not the product of our own age and culture; they come to us from a long past. But the invention of the machine has given them a power and scope they never had in the past from which they derive. Our law and politics and the incidents of human association depend upon a novel combination of the machine and money, and the result is the pecuniary culture characteristic of our civilization. The spiritual factor of our tradition, equal opportunity and free association and intercommunication, is obscured and crowded out. Instead of the development of individualities which it prophetically set forth, there is a perversion of the whole ideal of individualism to conform to the practices of a pecuniary culture. It has become the source and justification of inequalities and oppressions. Hence our compromises, and the conflicts in which aims and standards are confused beyond recognition.

Chapter II

"AMERICA"—BY FORMULA

WE HAVE HEARD a good deal of late years of class-consciousness. The phrase "nation-conscious" does not happen to be current, but present-day nationalism is an exacerbated expression of it in fact. A still more recent manifestation might be called "culture-consciousness" or "civilization-consciousness." Like class-consciousness and nationalism, it assumes an invidious form; it is an exponent—and a coefficient—of conflict between groups. The war and its consequences may not have produced in our own country a consciousness of "Americanism" as a distinctive mode of civilization, but they have definitely had that effect among the intellectual élite of Europe.

Americanism as a form of culture did not exist, before the war, for Europeans. Now it does exist and as a menace. In reaction and as a protest, there is developing, at least among literary folk, the consciousness of a culture which is distinctively European, something which is precious and whose very existence is threatened by an invasion of a new form of barbarism issuing from the United States. Acute hostility to a powerful alien influence is taking the place of complacent ignoring of what was felt to be negligible. It would take a wider knowledge than mine to list even the titles of books and articles coming yearly from the presses of Europe whose burden is the threat of "America" to the traditional culture of Europe.

I am not concerned here with the European side of the matter. Most social unifications come about in response to external pressure. The same is likely to be true of a United States of Europe. If the ideal is approximated in reality, it will probably be as a protective reaction to the economic and financial hegemony of the United States of America. The result would probably be a good thing for Europe, and thus unwittingly we should serve one good purpose, internationally speaking. But it is, in the end, no great consolation to know that in losing our own soul we have been a means of helping save the soul of someone else. Just what is the America whose picture is forming in the minds of European critics?

Some of the writers are ignorant as well as bitter. These may be neglected. Others are intelligent, as well informed as any foreigner can be about a foreign country, and not devoid of sympathy. Moreover, their judgments agree not only with one another but with the protests of native-born dissenters. For convenience and because of the straightforward intelligence of its author, I take as a point of departure the description of the American type of mind and character presented by Mueller Freienfels.* His treatment is the fairer because he understands by "American" a type of mind that is developing, from like causes, all over the world, and which would have emerged in time in Europe, even if there were no geographical America, although its development in the rest of the world

* "Mysteries of the Soul," translated from the German by Bernard Miall; New York, Knopf, 1929. It may be well to add, in view of the title, that there is nothing occult nor obscurantist about the book. By "soul" is meant "the manifold living reciprocal reactions between the self and the universe."

has been accelerated and intensified by the influence of this country.

As far as any actual American is true to the type that is proclaimed to be *the* American, he should be thrilled by the picture that is drawn of him. For we are told that the type is a genuine mutation in the history of culture; that it is new, the product of the last century, and that it is stamped with success. It is transforming the external conditions of life and thereby reacting on the psychical content of life; it is assimilating other types of itself and recoining them. No world-conquest, whether that of Rome or Christendom, compares with that of "Americanism" in extent or effectiveness. If success and quantity are in fact the standards of the "American," here are admissions that will content his soul. From the standpoint of the type depicted, he is approved; and what do adverse criticisms matter?

But either the type is not yet so definitely fixed as is represented, or else there are individual Americans who deviate from type. For there are many who will have reserves in their admiration of the picture that is presented. Of course

the dissenters may be, as the European critics
say, impotent sports, fish out of water and
affected with nostalgia for the European tradition. Nevertheless, it is worth while to raise the
question as to whether the American type, supposing there is to be one, has as yet taken on
definitive form. First, however, what are alleged
to be the characteristics of the type?

Fundamentally, they spring from impersonal-
ity. The roots of the intellect are unconscious
and vital, in instincts and emotions. In America,
we are told, this subconsciousness is disregarded;
it is suppressed or is subordinated to conscious
rationality, which means that it is adapted to the
needs and conditions of the external world. We
have "intellect," but distinctly in the Bergsonian
sense; mind attuned to the conditions of action
upon matter, upon the world. Our emotional life
is quick, excitable, undiscriminating, lacking in
individuality and in direction by intellectual life.
Hence the "externality and superficiality of the
American soul"; it has no ultimate inner unity
and uniqueness—no true personality.

The marks and signs of this "impersonaliza-
tion" of the human soul are quantification of

life, with its attendant disregard of quality; its mechanization and the almost universal habit of esteeming technique as an end, not as a means, so that organic and intellectual life is also "rationalized"; and, finally, standardization. Differences and distinctions are ignored and overridden; agreement, similarity, is the ideal. There is not only absence of social discrimination but of intellectual; critical thinking is conspicuous by its absence. Our pronounced trait is mass suggestibility. The adaptability and flexibility that we display in our practical intelligence when dealing with external conditions have found their way into our souls. Homogeneity of thought and emotion has become an ideal.

Quantification, mechanization and standardization: these are then the marks of the Americanization that is conquering the world. They have their good side; external conditions and the standard of living are undoubtedly improved. But their effects are not limited to these matters; they have invaded mind and character, and subdued the soul to their own dye. The criticism is familiar; it is so much the burden of our own critics that one is never quite sure how much of the picture of foreign critics is drawn from direct observation and how much from native novels and essays that are not complacent with the American scene. This fact does not detract from the force of the indictment; it rather adds to it, and raises the more insistently the question of what our life means.

I shall not deny the existence of these characteristics, nor of the manifold evils of superficialism and externalism that result in the production of intellectual and moral mediocrity. In the main these traits exist and they characterize American life and are already beginning to dominate that of other countries. But their import is another thing than their existence. Mueller Freienfels is intelligent enough to acknowledge that they are transitional rather than final. He recognizes that the forces are so intrinsic that it is foolish to rebel against them and lament the past. "The question is how we are to pass through them and transcend them." It is this note which distinguishes his appraisal from so many others.

In reply to the question, one may at least say

that we are still in an early stage of the transition. Anything that is at most but a hundred years old has hardly had time to disclose its meaning in the slow secular processes of human history. And it may be questioned whether even our author has not sometimes succumbed to the weakness of lesser critics in treating the passing symptoms as inherent characters. I do not have in mind here an "optimistic" appeal to future time and its possibilities. I rather wish to raise the question as to how many of the defects and evils that are supposed to belong to the present order are in fact projections into it of a departing past order.

Strength, power, is always relative, not absolute. Conquest is an exhibition of weakness in the conquered as well as of strength in the conqueror. Transitions are out of something as well as into something; they reveal a past as well as project a future. There must have been something profoundly awry in the quality, spirituality, and individualized variety of the past, or they would not have succumbed as readily as we are told they are doing to the quantification, mechanization and standardization of the present.

And the defective and perverse elements have certainly not been displaced. They survive in the present. Present conditions give these factors an opportunity to disclose themselves. They are not now kept under and out of sight. Their overt manifestation is not a cheering spectacle. But as long as they did not show themselves on a scale large enough to attract notice, they could not be dealt with. I wonder very much whether many of the things that are objected to in the present scene—and justly so—are not in fact revelations of what the older type of culture covered up, and whether their perceptible presence is not to be credited rather than debited to the forces that are now active.

It is possible of course to argue—as Keyserling for example seems to do—that the new or American order signifies simply that the animal instincts of man have been released, while the older European tradition kept them in disciplined subjection to something higher, called with pleasing vagueness "spirituality." The suspicion that suppression is not solution is not confined to America. Undue and indiscriminate greediness in the presence of accessible food may be a symptom of previous starvation rather than an inevitable exhibition of the old Adam. A culture whose tradition rests on depreciation of the flesh and on making a sharp difference between body and mind, instinct and reason, practice and theory, may have wrought corruption of flesh and degeneration of spirit. It would take a degree of wisdom no one possesses to tell just what, in the undesirable features of the present, is a reflection of an old but not as yet transformed system of life and thought, and how much is a genuine product of the new forces.

One thing seems to be reasonably certain. The prized and vaunted "individuality" of European culture that is threatened by the leveling standardization and uniformity of the American type was a very limited affair. If one were to retort in kind, one could ask how much share in it was had by the peasant and proletarian. And it is much more than a retort to say that a peasantry and proletariat which has been released from intellectual bondage will for a time have its revenge. Because there is no magic in democracy to confer immediately the power of critical discrimination upon the masses who have been outside any intellectual movement, and who have taken their morals and their religion from an external authority above them—an authority which science is destroying—it does not follow that the ineptitude of the many is the creation of democracy.

Take one instance—the present interest in technique, and the domination of the "American type" by technique. It will hardly be argued, I suppose, that the mere absence of technique—intelligent means and methods for securing results—is itself a mark of an intrinsically desirable civilization. Nor is it surprising that the discovery of the actuality and potentiality of technique in all branches of human life should have an immediately intoxicating effect. What is called the American mentality is characterized by this discovery, and by the exaggerations that come with the abruptness of the discovery. There is much to be said against quantification and standardization. But the discovery of competent technique stands on a different level. The world has not suffered from absence of ideals and spiritual aims anywhere nearly as much as it has suf-

fered from absence of means for realizing the
ends which it has prized in a literary and sentimental way. Technique is still a novelty in most
matters, and like most novelties is played with
for a while on its own account. But it will be used
for ends beyond itself some time; and I think
that interest in technique is precisely the thing
which is most promising in our civilization, the
thing which in the end will break down devotion
to external standardization and the mass-quan-
tity ideal. For its application has not gone far
as yet; and interest in it is still largely vicarious,
being that, so to say, of the spectator rather than
of naturalization in use. In the end, technique
can only signify emancipation of individuality,
and emancipation on a broader scale than has
obtained in the past.

In his most hopeful anticipation of a future to
which we may be moving, Freienfels calls attention to the fact that the impoverishment of
the individual is accompanied, even now, by an
enrichment of community resources. Collectively,
present society, he says, is marked by a power
over nature and by intellectual resource and
power exceeding that of the classic Athenian and

the man of the Renaissance. Why is it that this collective enrichment does not operate to elevate correspondingly the life of individuals? This question he does not ask. Failure to consider it constitutes to my mind the chief failure of critics whether foreign or native. Our materialism, our devotion to money making and to having a good time, are not things by themselves. They are the product of the fact that we live in a money culture; of the fact that our technique and technology are controlled by interest in private profit. There lies the serious and fundamental defect of our civilization, the source of the secondary and induced evils to which so much attention is given. Critics are dealing with symptoms and effects. The evasion of fundamental economic causes by critics both foreign and native seems to me to be an indication of the prevalence of the old European tradition, with its disregard for the body, material things, and practical concerns. The development of the American type, in the sense of the critics, is an expression of the fact that we have retained this tradition and the economic system of private gain on which it is based, while at the same time we have made an independent development of industry and technology that is nothing short of revolutionary. When our critics deal with this issue instead of avoiding it there will be something really doing.

Until the issue is met, the confusion of a civilization divided against itself will persist. The mass development, which our European critics tell us has submerged individuality, *is* the product of a machine age; in some form it will follow in all countries from the extension of a machine technology. Its immediate effect has been, without doubt, a subjection of certain types of individuality. As far as individuality is associated with aristocracy of the historic type, the extension of the machine age will presumably be hostile to individuality in its traditional sense all over the world. But the strictures of our European critics only define the issue touched upon in the previous chapter. The problem of constructing a new individuality consonant with the objective conditions under which we live is the deepest problem of our times.

There are two "solutions" that fail to solve. One of these is the method of avoidance. This

course is taken as far as it is assumed that the
only valid type of individuality is that which
holds over from the ages that anteceded machine
technology and the democratic society it creates.
The course that is complementary to the method
of escape springs from assumption that the present situation is final; that it presents something
inherently ultimate and fixed. Only as it is
treated as transitive and moving, as material to
be dealt with in shaping a later outcome, only,
that is, as it is treated as a *problem,* is the idea
of any solution genuine and relevant. We may
well take the formula advanced by European
critics as a means of developing our consciousness of some of the conditions of the problem. So
regarded, the problem is seen to be essentially
that of creation of a new individualism as significant for modern conditions as the old individualism at its best was for its day and place. The
first step in further definition of this problem is
realization of the collective age which we have
already entered. When that is apprehended, the
issue will define itself as utilization of the realities of a corporate civilization to validate and
embody the distinctive moral element in the

INDIVIDUALISM—OLD AND NEW

American version of individualism: Equality and freedom expressed not merely externally and politically but through personal participation in the development of a shared culture.

CHAPTER III

THE UNITED STATES, INCORPO-RATED

IT WAS NOT long ago that it was fashionable for both American and foreign observers of our national scene to sum up the phenomena of our social life under the title of "individualism." Some treated this alleged individualism as our distinctive achievement; some critics held that it was the source of our backwardness, the mark of a relatively uncivilized estate. To-day both interpretations seem equally inept and outmoded. Individualism is still carried on our banners and attempts are made to use it as a war cry, especially when it is desired to defeat governmental regulation of any form of industry previously exempt from legal control. Even in high quarters, rugged individualism is praised as the glory of American life. But such words have little relation to the moving facts of that life.

There is no word which adequately expresses what is taking place. "Socialism" has too specific political and economic associations to be appropriate. "Collectivism" is more neutral, but it, too, is a party-word rather than a descriptive term. Perhaps the constantly increasing rôle of corporations in our economic life gives a clue to a fitting name. The word may be used in a wider sense than is conveyed by its technical legal meaning. We may then say that the United States has steadily moved from an earlier pioneer individualism to a condition of dominant corporateness. The influence business corporations exercise in determining present industrial and economic activities is both a cause and a symbol of the tendency to combination in all phases of life. Associations tightly or loosely organized more and more define the opportunities, the choices and the actions of individuals.

I have said that the growth of legal corporations in manufacturing, transportation, distribution and finance is symbolic of the development of corporateness in all phases of life. The era of trust-busting is an almost forgotten age. Not only are big mergers the order of the day, but popular sentiment now looks upon them with pride rather than with fear. Size is our current measure of greatness in this as in other matters. It is not necessary to ask whether the opportunity for speculative manipulation for the sake of private gain, or increased public service at a lower cost, is the dominant motive. Personal motives hardly count as productive causes in comparison with impersonal forces. Mass production and mass distribution inevitably follow in the wake of an epoch of steam and electricity. These have created a common market, the parts of which are held together by intercommunication and interdependence; distance is eliminated and the tempo of action enormously accelerated. Aggregated capital and concentrated control are the contemporary responses.

Political control is needed, but the movement cannot be arrested by legislation. Witness the condition of nearly innocuous desuetude of the Sherman Anti-Trust Act. Newspapers, manufacturing plants, utilities supplying light, power and local transportation, banks, retail stores, theaters and the movies, have all joined in the movement toward integration. General Motors, the American Telegraph and Telephone Company, United States Steel, the rapid growth of chain-store systems, combinations of radio companies with companies controlling theaters all over the country, are familiar facts. Railway consolidations have been slowed up by politics and internal difficulties, but few persons doubt that they, too, are coming. The political control of the future to be effective must take a positive instead of negative form.

For the forces at work in this movement are too vast and complex to cease operation at the behest of legislation. Aside from direct evasions of laws, there are many legal methods of carrying the movement forward. Interlocking directorates, interpurchase of stocks by individuals and corporations, grouping into holding companies, investing companies with enough holdings to sway policies, effect the same end as do direct mergers. It was stated at a recent convention of bankers that eighty per cent of the capitalization of all the banks of the country is now in the hands of twelve financial concerns. It is evident that virtual control of the other twenty per cent, except for negligible institutions having only local importance, automatically ensues.

An economist could multiply instances and give them a more precise form. But I am not an economist, and the facts in any case are too well known to need detailed rehearsal. For my purpose is only to indicate the bearing of the development of these corporations upon the change of social life from an individual to a corporate affair. Reactions to the change are psychological, professional, political; they affect the working ideas, beliefs and conduct of all of us.

The sad decline of the farmer cannot be understood except in the light of the industrialization of the country which is coincident with its "corporization." The government is now going to try to do for the collectivizing of the agriculturists the sort of thing that business acumen has already done—temporarily against the desire of the government—for manufactures and transportation. The plight of the uncombined and unintegrated is proof of the extent to which the country is controlled by the corporate idea. Sociologists who concern themselves with rural life are now chiefly occupied with pointing out the influence of urban districts—that is, of those where industrial organization predominates—upon the determination of conditions in country districts.

There are other decays which tell the same story. The old-type artisan, trained by individual apprenticeship for skilled individual work, is disappearing. Mass production by men massed together to operate machines with their minute divisions of labor, is putting him out of business. In many cases, a few weeks at a machine give about all the education—or rather training—that is needed. Mass production causes a kind of mass education in which individual capacity and skill are submerged. While the artisan becomes more of a mechanic and less of an artist, those who are still called artists either put themselves, as writers and designers, at the disposal of organized business, or are pushed out to the edge as eccentric bohemians. The artist remains, one may say, as a surviving individual force, but the esteem in which the calling is socially held in this country measures the degree of his force. The status of the artist in any form of social life affords a fair measure of the state of its culture. The inorganic position of the artist in American life to-day is convincing evidence of what happens to the isolated individual who lives in a society growing corporate.

Attention has recently been called to a new phenomenon in human culture:—the business mind, having its own conversation and language, its own interests, its own intimate groupings in which men of this mind, in their collective capacity, determine the tone of society at large as well as the government of industrial society, and have more political influence than the government itself. I am not concerned here with their political power. The fact significant for present discussion is that we now have, although without formal or legal status, a mental and moral corporateness for which history affords no parallel. Our indigenous heroes are the Fords and Edisons who typify this mind to the public. Critics may find amusement in ridiculing Rotarians, Kiwanians and Lions, but the latter can well afford to disregard the ridicule because they are representatives of the dominant corporate mentality.

Nowhere is the decline of the old-fashioned

individual and individualism more marked than in leisure life, in amusements and sports. Our colleges only follow the movement of the day when they make athletics an organized business, aroused and conducted under paid directors in the spirit of pure collectivism. The formation of theater chains is at once the cause and the effect of the destruction of the older independent life of leisure carried on in separate homes. The radio, the movies, the motor car, all make for a common and aggregate mental and emotional life. With technical exceptions, to be found in special publications and in some portion of all newspapers, the press is the organ of amusement for a hurried leisure time, and it reflects and carries further the formation of mental collectivism by massed methods. Crime, too, is assuming a new form; it is organized and corporate.

Our apartments and our subways are signs of the invasion and decline of privacy. Private "rights" have almost ceased to have a definable meaning. We live exposed to the greatest flood of mass suggestion that any people has ever experienced. The need for united action, and the supposed need of integrated opinion and sentiment, are met by organized propaganda and advertising. The publicity agent is perhaps the most significant symbol of our present social life. There are individuals who resist; but, for a time at least, sentiment can be manufactured by mass methods for almost any person or any cause.

These things are not said to be deplored, nor even in order to weigh their merits and demerits. They are merely reported as indications of the nature of our social scene, of the extent to which it is formed and directed by corporate and collective factors toward collective ends. Coincident with these changes in mentality and prestige are basic, if hardly acknowledged, changes in the ideas by which life is interpreted. Industry, again, provides the striking symbols.

What has become of the old-fashioned ideal of thrift? Societies for the promotion of savings among the young were much hurt in their feelings when Henry Ford urged a free scale of expenditures instead of a close scale of personal savings. But his recommendation was in line with all the economic tendencies of the day. Speeded-up mass production demands increased buying.

INDIVIDUALISM—OLD AND NEW

It is promoted by advertising on a vast scale, by instalment selling, by agents skilled in breaking down sales resistance. Hence buying becomes an economic "duty" which is as consonant with the present epoch as thrift was with the period of individualism. For the industrial mechanism depends upon maintaining some kind of an equilibrium between production and consumption. If the equilibrium is disturbed, the whole social structure is affected and prosperity ceases to have a meaning. Replacement and extension of capital are indeed more required than they ever were. But the savings of individuals, as such, are petty and inadequate to the task. New capital is chiefly supplied by the surplus earnings of big corporate organizations, and it becomes meaningless to tell individual buyers that industry can be kept going only by their abstinence from the enjoyments of consumption. The old plea for "sacrifice" loses its force. In effect, the individual is told that by indulging in the enjoyment of free purchasing he performs his economic duty, transferring his surplus income to the corporate store where it can be most effectively used. Virtue departs from mere thrift.

The corresponding change in the ruling conceptions of the older economic theory is, of course, the obligation upon employers to pay high wages. Growing consumption through increased expenditure that effects a still greater amount of production cannot be maintained unless consumers have the wherewithal. The consumption demand of the well-to-do is limited; and their number is limited. Purchase of luxuries by this class has, indeed, become a necessity rather than a vice, since it helps to keep moving the wheels of industry and commerce. Luxury may still be condemned as a vice, just as old habits still show themselves in approving thrift as a virtue. But the condemnation is almost an idle beating of the air, because it goes contrary to the movement of industry and trade. In any case, however, there is a definite limit to the consumption of luxuries, as well as of what used to be called necessary commodities, on the part of the wealthy. The demands that make production and distribution "going concerns" must come from the mass of the people, that is, from workers and those in subordinate salaried positions. Hence the "new economy" based on the idea of the identity of high wages with industrial prosperity.

It is difficult, perhaps impossible, to measure the full import of this revaluation of those concepts of saving and low wages which were basic in the older doctrine. If it merely expressed a change in abstract economic theory, its significance would not be great. But the change in theory is itself a reflex of a social change which is hardly less than revolutionary. I do not mean that I think that the "new economy" is firmly established as a fact, or that the endless chain of speeding up mass consumption in order to speed up production is either endless or entirely logical. But certain changes do not go backward. Those who have enjoyed high wages and a higher standard of consumption will not be content to return to a lower level. A new condition has been created with which we shall have to reckon constantly in the future. Depressions and slumps will come, but they can never be treated in the future in the casual and fatalistic way in which they have been accepted in the past. They will appear abnormal instead of normal, and society, including the industrial captains, will have to

UNITED STATES, INCORPORATED

assume a responsibility from which it and they were previously exempt. The gospel of general prosperity in this life will have to meet tests to which that of salvation in the next world, as a compensation for the miseries of this one, was not subjected. "Prosperity" is not such an assured fact in 1930 as it seemed to many to be in the earlier part of 1929. The slump or the depression makes the problem caused by the growth of corporate industry and finance the more acute. An excess income of eight billions a year will only aggravate the economic situation unless it can find outlet in productive channels. It cannot do this unless consumption is sustained. This cannot happen unless organization and control extend from production and distribution to consumption. The alternatives seem to be either a definite expansion of social corporateness to include the average consumer or else economic suffering on a vast scale.

I have said that the instances cited of the reaction of the growing corporateness of society upon social mind and habit were not given in order to be either deplored or approved. They are set forth only to call out the picture of the decline of an individualistic philosophy of life, and the formation of a collectivistic scheme of interdependence, which finds its way into every cranny of life, personal, intellectual, emotional, affecting leisure as well as work, morals as well as economics. But because the purpose was to indicate the decay of the older conceptions, although they are still those that are most loudly and vocally professed, the illustrations given inevitably emphasize those features of growing standardization and mass uniformity which critics justly deplore. It would be unfair, accordingly, to leave the impression that these traits are the whole of the story of the "corporization" of American life.

The things which are criticized are the outward signs of an inner movement toward integration on a scale never known before. "Socialization" is not wholly a eulogistic term nor a desirable process. It involves danger to some precious values; it involves a threat of danger to some things which we should not readily lose. But in spite of much cant which is talked about "service" and "social responsibility," it marks the beginning of a new era of integration. What its ultimate possibilities are, and to what extent these possibilities will be realized, is for the future to tell. The need of the present is to apprehend the fact that, for better or worse, we are living in a corporate age.

It is of the nature of society as of life to contain a balance of opposed forces. Actions and reactions are ultimately equal and counterpart. At present the "socialization" is largely mechanical and quantitative. The system is kept in a kind of precarious balance by the movement toward lawless and reckless overstimulation among individuals. If the chaos and the mechanism are to generate a mind and soul, an integrated personality, it will have to be an intelligence, a sentiment and an individuality of a new type.

Meanwhile, the lawlessness and irregularity (and I have in mind not so much outward criminality as emotional instability and intellectual confusion) and the uniform standardization are two sides of the same emerging corporate society. Hence only in an external sense does society maintain a balance. When the corporateness becomes internal, when, that is, it is realized in thought and purpose, it will become qualitative. In this change, law will be realized not as a rule arbitrarily imposed from without but as the relations which hold individuals together. The balance of the individual and the social will be organic. The emotions will be aroused and satisfied in the course of normal living, not in abrupt deviations to secure the fulfillment which is denied them in a situation which is so incomplete that it cannot be admitted into the affections and yet is so pervasive that it cannot be escaped: a situation which defines an individual divided within himself.

Chapter IV

THE LOST INDIVIDUAL

THE DEVELOPMENT OF a civilization that is outwardly corporate—or rapidly becoming so—has been accompanied by a submergence of the individual. Just how far this is true of the individual's opportunities in action, how far initiative and choice in what an individual does are restricted by the economic forces that make for consolidation, I shall not attempt to say. It is arguable that there has been a diminution of the range of decision and activity for the many along with exaggeration of opportunity of personal expression for the few. It may be contended that no one class in the past has the power now possessed by an industrial oligarchy. On the other hand, it may be held that this power of the few is, with respect to genuine individuality, specious; that those outwardly in control are in reality as much carried by forces external to themselves as are the many; that in fact these forces impel them into a common mold to such an extent that individuality is suppressed.

What is here meant by "the lost individual" is, however, so irrelevant to this question that it is not necessary to decide between the two views. For by it is meant a moral and intellectual fact which is independent of any manifestation of power in action. The significant thing is that the loyalties which once held individuals, which gave them support, direction, and unity of outlook on life, have well-nigh disappeared. In consequence, individuals are confused and bewildered. It would be difficult to find in history an epoch as lacking in solid and assured objects of belief and approved ends of action as is the present. Stability of individuality is dependent upon stable objects to which allegiance firmly attaches itself. There are, of course, those who are still militantly fundamentalist in religious and social creed. But their very clamor is evidence that the tide is set against them. For the others, traditional objects of loyalty have become hollow or are openly repudiated, and they drift without sure anchorage. Individuals vibrate between a past that is intellectually too empty to give stability and a present that is too diversely crowded and chaotic to afford balance or direction to ideas and emotion.

Assured and integrated individuality is the product of definite social relationships and publicly acknowledged functions. Judged by this standard, even those who seem to be in control, and to carry the expression of their special individual abilities to a high pitch, are submerged. They may be captains of finance and industry, but until there is some consensus of belief as to the meaning of finance and industry in civilization as a whole, they cannot be captains of their own souls—their beliefs and aims. They exercise leadership surreptitiously and, as it were, absentmindedly. They lead, but it is under cover of impersonal and socially undirected economic forces. Their reward is found not in what they do, in their social office and function, but in a deflection of social consequences to private gain. They receive the acclaim and command the envy and admiration of the crowd, but the crowd is also composed of private individuals who are equally lost to a sense of social bearings and uses.

The explanation is found in the fact that while the actions promote corporate and collective results, these results are outside their intent and irrelevant to that reward of satisfaction which comes from a sense of social fulfillment. To themselves and to others, their business is private and its outcome is private profit. No complete satisfaction is possible where such a split exists. Hence the absence of a sense of social value is made up for by an exacerbated acceleration of the activities that increase private advantage and power. One cannot look into the inner consciousness of his fellows; but if there is any general degree of inner contentment on the part of those who form our pecuniary oligarchy, the evidence is sadly lacking. As for the many, they are impelled hither and yon by forces beyond their control.

The most marked trait of present life, economically speaking, is insecurity. It is tragic that millions of men desirous of working should be recurrently out of employment; aside from cyclical depressions there is a standing army at all times who have no regular work. We have not any adequate information as to the number of these persons. But the ignorance even as to numbers is slight compared with our inability to grasp the psychological and moral consequences of the precarious condition in which vast multitudes live. Insecurity cuts deeper and extends more widely than bare unemployment. Fear of loss of work, dread of the oncoming of old age, create anxiety and eat into self-respect in a way that impairs personal dignity. Where fears abound, courageous and robust individuality is undermined. The vast development of technological resources that might bring security in its train has actually brought a new mode of insecurity, as mechanization displaces labor. The mergers and consolidations that mark a corporate age are beginning to bring uncertainty into the economic lives of the higher salaried class, and that tendency is only just in its early stage. Realization that honest and industrious pursuit of a calling or business will not guarantee any stable level of life lessens respect for work and stirs large numbers to take a chance of some adventitious way of getting the wealth that will make security possible: witness the orgies of the stock-market in recent days.

The unrest, impatience, irritation and hurry that are so marked in American life are inevitable accompaniments of a situation in which individuals do not find support and contentment in the fact that they are sustaining and sustained members of a social whole. They are evidence, psychologically, of abnormality, and it is as idle to seek for their explanation within the deliberate intent of individuals as it is futile to think that they can be got rid of by hortatory moral appeal. Only an acute maladjustment between individuals and the social conditions under which they live can account for such widespread pathological phenomena. Feverish love of anything as long as it is a change which is distracting, impatience, unsettlement, nervous discontentment, and desire for excitement, are not native to human nature. They are so abnormal as to demand explanation in some deep-seated cause.

I should explain a seeming hypocrisy on the same ground. We are not consciously insincere in our professions of devotion to ideals of "service"; they mean something. Neither the Rotarian nor the big business enterprise uses the term merely as a cloak for "putting something over"

which makes for pecuniary gain. But the lady
doth protest too much. The wide currency of
such professions testifies to a sense of a social
function of business which is expressed in words
because it is so lacking in fact, and yet which is
felt to be rightfully there. If our external combinations in industrial activity were reflected in
organic integrations of the desires, purposes and
satisfactions of individuals, the verbal protesta-
tions would disappear, because social utility
would be a matter of course.

Some persons hold that a genuine mental counterpart of the outward social scheme is actually
forming. Our prevailing mentality, our "ideology," is said to be that of the "business mind"
which has become so deplorably pervasive. Are
not the prevailing standards of value those
derived from pecuniary success and economic
prosperity? Were the answer unqualifiedly in
the affirmative, we should have to admit that our
outer civilization is attaining an inner culture
which corresponds to it, however much we might
disesteem the quality of that culture. The objec-
tion that such a condition is impossible, since man
cannot live by bread, by material prosperity,

alone, is tempting, but it may be said to beg the question. The conclusive answer is that the business mind is not itself unified. It is divided within itself and must remain so as long as the results of industry as the determining force in life are corporate and collective while its animating motives and compensations are so unmitigatedly private. A unified mind, even of the business type, can come into being only when conscious intent and consummation are in harmony with consequences actually effected. This statement expresses conditions so psychologically assured that it may be termed a law of mental integrity. Proof of the existence of the split is found in the fact that while there is much planning of future development with a view to dividends within large business corporations, there is no corresponding coördinated planning of social development.

The growth of corporateness is arbitrarily restricted. Hence it operates to limit individuality, to put burdens on it, to confuse and submerge it. It crowds more out than it incorporates in an ordered and secure life. It has made rural districts stagnant while bringing excess and restless movement to the city. The restriction of corporateness lies in the fact that it remains on the cash level. Men are brought together on the one side by investment in the same joint stock company, and on the other hand by the fact that the machine compels mass production in order that investors may get their profits. The results affect all society in all its phases. But they are as inorganic as the ultimate human motives that operate are private and egoistic. An economic individualism of motives and aims underlies our present corporate mechanisms, and undoes the individual.

The loss of individuality is conspicuous in the economic region because our civilization is so predominantly a business civilization. But the fact is even more obvious when we turn to the political scene. It would be a waste of words to expatiate on the meaninglessness of present political platforms, parties and issues. The old-time slogans are still reiterated, and to a few these words still seem to have a real meaning. But it is too evident to need argument that on the whole our politics, as far as they are not covertly manipulated in behalf of the pecuniary advantage of groups, are in a state of confusion; issues are improvised from week to week with a constant shift of allegiance. It is impossible for individuals to find themselves politically with surety and efficiency under such conditions. Political apathy broken by recurrent sensations and spasms is the natural outcome.

The lack of secure objects of allegiance, without which individuals are lost, is especially striking in the case of the liberal. The liberalism of the past was characterized by the possession of a definite intellectual creed and program; that was its distinction from conservative parties which needed no formulated outlook beyond defense of things as they were. In contrast, liberals operated on the basis of a thought-out social philosophy, a theory of politics sufficiently definite and coherent to be easily translated into a program of policies to be pursued. Liberalism to-day is hardly more than a temper of mind, vaguely called forward-looking, but quite uncertain as to where to look and what to look forward to. For many individuals, as well as in its social results, this fact is hardly less than a tragedy. The tragedy may be unconscious for the mass, but they show its reality in their aimless drift, while the more thoughtful are consciously disturbed. For human nature is self-possessed only as it has objects to which it can attach itself.

I do not think it is fantastic to connect our excited and rapacious nationalism with the situation in which corporateness has gone so far as to detach individuals from their old local ties and allegiances but not far enough to give them a new center and order of life. The most militaristic of nations secures the loyalty of its subjects not by physical force but through the power of ideas and emotions. It cultivates ideals of loyalty, of solidarity, and common devotion to a common cause. Modern industry, technology and commerce have created modern nations in their external form. Armies and navies exist to protect commerce, to make secure the control of raw materials, and to command markets. Men would not sacrifice their lives for the purpose of securing economic gain for a few if the conditions presented themselves to their minds in this bald fashion. But the balked demand for genuine coöperativeness and reciprocal solidarity in daily life finds an outlet in nationalistic sentiment. Men have a pathetic instinct toward the adventure of living and struggling together; if the daily community does not feed this impulse, the romantic imagination pictures a grandiose nation in which all are one. If the simple duties of peace do not establish a common life, the emotions are mobilized in the service of a war that will supply its temporary simulation.

I have thus far made no reference to what many persons would consider the most serious and the most overtly evident of all the modes of loss of secure objects of loyalty—religion. It is probably easy to exaggerate the extent of the decadence of religion in an outward sense, church membership, church-going and so on. But it is hardly possible to overstate its decline as a vitally integrative and directive force in men's thought and sentiments. Whether even in the ages of the past that are called religious, religion was itself the actively central force that it is sometimes said to have been may be doubted. But it cannot be doubted that it was the symbol of the existence of conditions and forces that gave unity and a center to men's views of life. It at least gathered together in weighty and shared symbols a sense of the objects to which men were so attached as to have support and stay in their outlook on life.

Religion does not now effect this result. The divorce of church and state has been followed by that of religion and society. Wherever religion has not become a merely private indulgence, it has become at best a matter of sects and denominations divided from one another by doctrinal differences, and united internally by tenets that have a merely historical origin, and a purely metaphysical or else ritualistic meaning. There is no such bond of social unity as once united Greeks, Romans, Hebrews, and Catholic medieval Europe.' There are those who realize what is portended by the loss of religion as an integrating bond. Many of them despair of its recovery through the development of social values to which the imagination and sentiments of individuals can attach themselves with intensity. They wish to reverse the operation and to form the social bond of unity and of allegiance by regeneration of the isolated individual soul.

Aside from the fact that there is no consensus as to what a new religious attitude is to center itself about, the injunction puts the cart before the horse. Religion is not so much a root of unity as it is its flower or fruit. The very attempt to secure integration for the individual, and through him for society, by means of a deliberate and conscious cultivation of religion, is itself proof of how far the individual has become lost through detachment from acknowledged social values. It is no wonder that when the appeal does not take the form of dogmatic fundamentalism, it tends to terminate in either some form of esoteric occultism or private estheticism. The sense of wholeness which is urged as the essence of religion can be built up and sustained only through membership in a society which has attained a degree of unity. The attempt to cultivate it first in individuals and then extend it to form an organically unified society is fantasy. Indulgence in this fantasy infects such interpretations of American life as are found, to take one signal example, in Waldo Frank's * "The Rediscovery

* After a brilliant exposition of the dissolution of the European synthesis, he goes on to say "man's need of order and his making of order are his science, his art, his religion; and these are all to be referred to the initial sense of order called the self," quite oblivious of the fact that this doctrine of the primacy of the self is precisely a reaction of the romantic and subjective age to the dissolution he has depicted, having its meaning only in that dissolution.

of America." It marks a manner of yearning and not a principle of construction.

For the idea that the outward scene is chaotic because of the machine, which is a principle of chaos, and that it will remain so until individuals reinstitute wholeness within themselves, simply reverses the true state of things. The outward scene, if not fully organized, is relatively so in the corporateness which the machine and its technology have produced; the inner man is the jungle which can be subdued to order only as the forces of organization at work in externals are reflected in corresponding patterns of thought, imagination and emotion. The sick cannot heal themselves by means of their disease, and disintegrated individuals can achieve unity only as the dominant energies of community life are incorporated to form their minds. If these energies were, in reality, mere strivings for private pecuniary gain, the case would indeed be hopeless. But they are constituted by a collective art of technology, which individuals merely deflect to their private ends. There are the beginnings of an objective order through which individuals may get their bearings.

INDIVIDUALISM—OLD AND NEW

Conspicuous signs of the disintegration of individuality due to failure to reconstruct the self so as to meet the realities of present social life have not been mentioned. In a census that was taken among leaders of opinion concerning the urgency of present social problems, the state of law, the courts, lawlessness and criminality stood at the head of the list, and by a considerable distance. We are even more emphatically than when Kipling wrote the words, the people that make "the laws they flout, and flout the laws they make." We combine an ardor unparalleled in history for "passing" laws with a casual and deliberate disregard for them when they are on the statute books. We believe—to judge by our legislative actions—that we can create morals by law (witness the prohibition amendment for an instance on a large scale) and neglect the fact that all laws except those which regulate technical procedures are registrations of existing social customs and their attendant moral habits and purposes. I can, however, only think of this phenomenon as a symptom, not as a cause. It is a natural expression of a period in which changes in the structure of society have dissolved old bonds and allegiances. We attempt to make good this social relaxation and dissolution by legal enactments, while the actual disintegration discloses itself in the lawlessness which reveals the artificial character of this method of securing social integrity.

Volumes could be formed by collecting articles and editorials written about relaxation of traditional moral codes. A movement has caught public attention, which, having for some obscure reason assumed the name "humanism," proposes restraint and moderation, exercised in and by the higher volition of individuals, as the solution of our ills. It finds that naturalism as practiced by artists and mechanism as taught by philosophers who take their clew from natural science, have broken down the inner laws and imperatives which can alone bring order and loyalty. I should be glad to be able to believe that artists and intellectuals have any such power in their hands; if they had, after using it to bring evil to society, they might change face and bring healing to it. But a sense of fact, together with a sense of humor, forbids the acceptance of any such belief. Literary persons and academic thinkers are now, more than ever, effects, not causes. They reflect and voice the disintegration which new modes of living, produced by new forms of industry and commerce, have introduced. They give witness to the unreality that has overtaken traditional codes in the face of the impact of new forces; indirectly, they proclaim the need of some new synthesis. But this synthesis can be humanistic only as the new conditions are themselves taken into account and are converted into the instrumentalities of a free and humane life. I see no way to "restrain" or turn back the industrial revolution and its consequences. In the absence of such a restraint (which would be efficacious if only it could occur), the urging of some inner restraint through the exercise of the higher personal will, whatever that may be, is itself only a futile echo of just the old individualism that has so completely broken down.

There are many phases of life which illustrate to anyone who chooses to think in terms of realities instead of words the utter irrelevance of the proposed remedy to actual conditions. One might take the present estate of amusements, of the movies, the radio, and organized vicarious sport, and ask just how this powerful eruption in which the resources of technology are employed for economic profit is to be met by the application of the inner *frein* or brake. Perhaps the most striking instance is found in the disintegration due to changes in family life and sex morale. It was not deliberate human intention that undermined the traditional household as the center of industry and education and as the focus of moral training; that sapped the older institution of enduring marriage. To ask the individuals who suffer the consequences of the general undermining and sapping to put an end to the consequences by acts of personal volition is merely to profess faith in moral magic. Recovery of individuals capable of stable and effective self-control can be had only as there is first a humbler exercise of will to observe existing social realities and to direct them according to their own potentialities.

Instances of the flux in which individuals are loosened from the ties that once gave order and support to their lives are glaring. They are indeed so glaring that they blind our eyes to the causes which produce them. Individuals are groping their way through situations which they do not direct and which do not give them direction. The beliefs and ideals that are uppermost in their consciousness are not relevant to the society in which they outwardly act and which constantly reacts upon them. Their conscious ideas and standards are inherited from an age that has passed away; their minds, as far as consciously entertained principles and methods of interpretation are concerned, are at odds with actual conditions. This profound split is the cause of distraction and bewilderment.

Individuals will refind themselves only as their ideas and ideals are brought into harmony with the realities of the age in which they act. The task of attaining this harmony is not an easy one. But it is more negative than it seems. If we could inhibit the principles and standards that are merely traditional, if we could slough off the opinions that have no living relationship to the situations in which we live, the unavowed forces that now work upon us unconsciously but unremittingly would have a chance to build minds after their own pattern, and individuals might, in consequence, find themselves in possession of objects to which imagination and emotion would stably attach themselves.

I do not mean, however, that the process of rebuilding can go on automatically. Discrimination is required in order to detect the beliefs and institutions that dominate merely because of custom and inertia, and in order to discover the moving realities of the present. Intelligence must distinguish, for example, the tendencies of the technology which produce the new corporateness from those inheritances proceeding out of the individualism of an earlier epoch which arrest and divide the operation of the new dynamics. It is difficult for us to conceive of individualism except in terms of stereotypes derived from former centuries. Individualism has been identified with ideas of initiative and invention that are bound up with private and exclusive economic gain. As long as this conception possesses our minds, the ideal of harmonizing our thought and desire with the realities of present social conditions will be interpreted to mean accommodation and surrender. It will even be understood to signify rationalization of the evils of existing society. A stable recovery of individuality waits upon an elimination of the older economic and political individualism, an elimination which will liberate imagination and endeavor for the task of making corporate society contribute to the free culture of its members. Only by economic revision can the sound element in the older individualism—equality of opportunity—be made a reality.

It is the part of wisdom to note the double meaning of such ideas as "acceptance." There is an acceptance that is of the intellect; it signifies facing facts for what they are. There is another acceptance that is of the emotions and will; that involves commitment of desire and effort. So far are the two from being identical that acceptance in the first sense is the precondition of all intelligent refusal of acceptance in the second sense. There is a prophetic aspect to all observation; we can perceive the meaning of what exists only as we forecast the consequences it entails. When a situation is as confused and divided within itself as is the present social estate, choice is implicated in observation. As one perceives different tendencies and different possible consequences, preference inevitably goes out to one or the other. Because acknowledgment in thought brings with it intelligent discrimination and choice, it is the first step out of confusion, the first step in forming those objects of significant allegiance out of which stable and efficacious individuality may grow. It might even perform the miracle of rendering conservatism relevant and thoughtful. It certainly is the prerequisite of an anchored liberalism.

CHAPTER V

TOWARD A NEW INDIVIDUALISM

OUR MATERIAL CULTURE, as anthropologists would call it, is verging upon the collective and corporate. Our moral culture, along with our ideology, is, on the other hand, still saturated with ideal and values of an individualism derived from the prescientific, pretechnological age. Its spiritual roots are found in medieval religion, which asserted the ultimate nature of the individual soul and centered the drama of life about the destiny of that soul. Its institutional and legal concepts were framed in the feudal period.

This moral and philosophical individualism anteceded the rise of modern industry and the era of the machine. It was the context in which the latter operated. The apparent subordination of the individual to established institutions often conceals from recognition the vital existence of a deep-seated individualism. But the fact that the controlling institution was the Church should remind us that in ultimate intent it existed to secure the salvation of the individual. That this individual was conceived as a soul, and that the end served by the institution was deferred to another and everlasting life conceal from contemporary realization the underlying individualism. In its own time, its substance consisted in just this eternal spiritual character of the personal soul; the power of the established institutions proceeded from their being the necessary means of accomplishing the supreme end of the individual.

The early phase of the industrial revolution wrought a great transformation. It gave a secular and worldly turn to the career of the individual, and it liquefied the static property concepts of feudalism by the shift of emphasis from agriculture to manufacturing. Still, the idea persisted that property and reward were intrinsically individual. There were, it is true, incompatible elements in the earlier and later versions of individualism. But a fusion of individual capitalism, of natural rights, and of morals founded in strictly individual traits and values remained, under the influence of Protestantism, the dominant intellectual synthesis.

The basis of this synthesis was destroyed, however, by the later development of the industrial system, which brought about the merging of personal capacity, effort and work into collective wholes. Meanwhile, the control of natural energies eliminated time and distance, so that action once adapted to local conditions was swallowed up in complex undertakings of indefinite extent. Yet the older mental equipment remained after its causes and foundations had disappeared. This, fundamentally, is the inner division out of which spring our present confusion and insincerities.

The earlier economic individualism had a definite creed and function. It sought to release from legal restrictions man's wants and his efforts to satisfy those wants. It believed that such emancipation would stimulate latent energy into action, would automatically assign individual ability to the work for which it was suited, would cause it to perform that work under stimulus of the advantage to be gained, and would secure for capacity and enterprise the reward and position to which they were entitled. At the same time, individual energy and savings would be serving the needs of others, and thus promoting the general welfare and effecting a general harmony of interests.

We have gone a long way since this philosophy was formulated. To-day, the most stalwart defenders of this type of individualism do not venture to repeat its optimistic assertions. At most, they are content to proclaim its consistency with unchanging human nature—which is said to be moved to effort only by the hope of personal gain—and to paint dire pictures of the inevitable consequences of change to any other régime. They ascribe all the material benefits of our present civilization to this individualism—as if machines were made by the desire for money profit, not by impersonal science; and as if they were driven by money alone, and not by electricity and steam under the direction of a collective technology.

In America, the older individualism assumed a romantic form. It was hardly necessary to elaborate a theory which equated personal gain with social advance. The demands of the practical situation called for the initiative, enterprise and vigor of individuals in all immediate work that urgently asked for doing, and their operation furthered the national life. The spirit of the time is expressed by Dr. Crothers, whose words Mr. Sims has appropriately taken for part of the text of his "Adventurous America":

"If you would understand the driving power of America, you must understand 'the divers discontented and impatient young men' who in each generation have found an outlet for their energy. . . . The noises which disturb you are not the cries of an angry proletariat, but are the shouts of eager young people who are finding new opportunities. . . . They represent to-day the enthusiasm of a new generation. They represent the Oregons and Californias toward which sturdy pioneers are moving undisturbed by obstacles. This is what the social unrest means in America."

If that is not an echo of the echo of a voice of long ago, I do not know what it is. I do not, indeed, hear the noises of an angry proletariat; but I should suppose the sounds heard are the murmurs of lost opportunities, along with the din of machinery, motor cars and speakeasies, by which the murmurs of discontent are drowned, rather than shouts of eagerness for adventurous opportunity.

The European version of the older individualism had its value and temporal justification because the new technology needed liberation from vexatious legal restrictions. Machine industry was itself in a pioneer condition, and those who carried it forward against obstacles of lethargy, skepticism and political obstruction were deserving of special reward. Moreover, accumulation of capital was thought of in terms of enterprises that to-day would be petty; there was no dream of the time when it would reach such a mass that it would determine the legal and political order. Poverty had previously been accepted as a dispensation of nature that was inevitable. The new industry promised a way out, at least to those possessed of energy and will to save and accumulate. But there was no anticipation of a time when the development of machine technology would afford the material basis for reasonable ease and comfort and of extensive leisure for all.

INDIVIDUALISM—OLD AND NEW

The shift that makes the older individualism a dying echo is more marked as well as more rapid in this country. Where is the wilderness which now beckons creative energy and affords untold opportunity to initiative and vigor? Where is the pioneer who goes forth rejoicing, even in the midst of privation, to its conquest? The wilderness exists in the movie and the novel; and the children of the pioneers, who live in the midst of surroundings artificially made over by the machine, enjoy pioneer life idly in the vicarious film. I see little social unrest which is the straining of energy for outlet in action; I find rather the protest against a weakening of vigor and a sapping of energy that emanate from the absence of constructive opportunity; and I see a confusion that is an expression of the inability to find a secure and morally rewarding place in a troubled and tangled economic scene.

Because of the bankruptcy of the older individualism, those who are aware of the breakdown often speak and argue as if individualism were itself done and over with. I do not suppose that those who regard socialism and individualism as antithetical really mean that individuality is going to die out or that it is not something intrinsically precious. But in speaking as if the only individualism were the local episode of the last two centuries, they play into the hands of those who would keep it alive in order to serve their own ends, and they slur over the chief problem—that of remaking society to serve the growth of a new type of individual. There are many who believe that socialism of some form is needed to realize individual initiative and security on a wide scale. They are concerned about the restriction of power and freedom to a few in the present régime, and they think that collective social control is necessary, at least for a time, in order to achieve its advantages for all. But they too often seem to assume that the result will be merely an extension of the earlier individualism to the many.

Such thinking treats individualism as if it were something static, having a uniform content. It ignores the fact that the mental and moral structure of individuals, the pattern of their desires and purposes, change with every great change in social constitution. Individuals who are not bound together in associations, whether domestic, economic, religious, political, artistic or educational, are monstrosities. It is absurd to suppose that the ties which hold them together are merely external and do not react into mentality and character, producing the framework of personal disposition.

The tragedy of the "lost individual" is due to the fact that while individuals are now caught up into a vast complex of associations, there is no harmonious and coherent reflection of the import of these connections into the imaginative and emotional outlook on life. This fact is of course due in turn to the absence of harmony within the state of society. There is an undoubted circle. But it is a vicious circle only as far as men decline to accept—in the intellectual, observing and inquiring spirit defined in the previous chapter—the realities of the social estate, and because of this refusal either surrender to the division or seek to save their individuality by escape or sheer emotional revolt. The habit of opposing the corporate and collective to the individual tends to the persistent continuation of the confusion and uncertainty. It distracts attention

TOWARD A NEW INDIVIDUALISM

from the crucial issue: How shall the individual refind himself in an unprecedentedly new social situation, and what qualities will the new individualism exhibit?

That the problem is not merely one of extending to all individuals the traits of economic initiative, opportunity and enterprise; that it is one of forming a new psychological and moral type, is suggested by the great pressure now brought to bear to effect conformity and standardization of American opinion. Why should regimentation, the erection of an average struck from the opinions of large masses into regulative norms, and in general the domination of quantity over quality, be so characteristic of present American life? I see but one fundamental explanation. The individual cannot remain intellectually a vacuum. If his ideas and beliefs are not the spontaneous function of a communal life in which he shares, a seeming censensus will be secured as a substitute by artificial and mechanical means. In the absence of mentality that is congruous with the new social corporateness that is coming into being, there is a desperate effort to fill the void

83

by external agencies which obtain a factitious agreement.

In consequence, our uniformity of thought is much more superficial than it seems to be. The standardization is deplorable, but one might almost say that one of the reasons it is deplorable is because it does not go deep. It goes far enough to effect suppression of original quality of thought, but not far enough to achieve enduring unity. Its superficial character is evident in its instability. All agreement of thought obtained by external means, by repression and intimidation, however subtle, and by calculated propaganda and publicity, is of necessity superficial; and whatever is superficial is in continual flux. The methods employed produce mass credulity, and this jumps from one thing to another according to the dominant suggestions of the day. We think and feel alike—but only for a month or a season. Then comes some other sensational event or personage to exercise a hypnotizing uniformity of response. At a given time, taken in cross-section, conformity is the rule. In a time span, taken longitudinally, instability and flux dominate. . . . I suppose there are others who have a feeling of irritation at such terms as "radio-conscious" and "air-minded," now so frequently forced upon us. I do not think the irritation is wholly due to linguistic causes. It testifies to a half-conscious sense of the external ways in which our minds are formed and swayed and of the superficiality and inconsistency of the result.

There are, I suppose, those who fancy that the emphasis which I put upon the corporateness of existing society in the United States is in effect, even if not in the writer's conscious intent, a plea for greater conformity than now exists. Nothing could be further from the truth. Identification of society with a level, whatever it be, high as well as low, of uniformity is just another evidence of that distraction because of which the individual is lost. Society is of course but the relations of individuals to one another in this form and that. And all relations are interactions, not fixed molds. The particular interactions that compose a human society include the give and take of participation, of a sharing that increases, that expands and deepens, the capacity and significance of the interacting factors. Conformity is a name for the absence of vital interplay; the arrest and benumbing of communication. As I have been trying to say, it is the artificial substitute used to hold men together in lack of associations that are incorporated into inner dispositions of thought and desire. I often wonder what meaning is given to the term "society" by those who oppose it to the intimacies of personal intercourse, such as those of friendship. Presumably they have in their minds a picture of rigid institutions or some set and external organization. But an institution that is other than the structure of human contact and intercourse is a fossil of some past society; organization, as in any living organism, is the coöperative consensus of multitudes of cells, each living in exchange with others.

I should suppose that the more intelligent of those who wield the publicity agencies which produce conformity would be disturbed at beholding their own success. I can easily understand that they should have a cynical sense of their ability to obtain the results they want at a given time; but I should think they would fear that likemindedness might, at a critical juncture, veer in an unexpected direction and turn with equal unanimity against the things and interests it has been manipulated to support. Crowd psychology is dangerous in its instability. To rely upon it for permanent support is playing with a fire that may get out of control. Conformity is enduringly effective when it is a spontaneous and largely unconscious manifestation of the agreements that spring from genuine communal life. An artificially induced uniformity of thought and sentiment is a symptom of an inner void. Not all of it that now exists is intentionally produced; it is not the result of deliberate manipulation. But it is, on the other hand, the result of causes so external as to be accidental and precarious.

The "joining" habit of the average American, and his excessive sociability, may well have an explanation like that of conformity. They, too, testify to nature's abhorrence of that vacuum which the passing of the older individualism has produced. We should not be so averse to solitude if we had, when we were alone, the companionship of communal thought built into our mental habits. In the absence of this communion, there is the need for reinforcement by external contact. Our sociability is largely an effort to find substitutes for that normal consciousness of connection and union that proceeds from being a sustained and sustaining member of a social whole.

Just as the new individualism cannot be achieved by extending the benefits of the older economic individualism to more persons, so it cannot be obtained by a further development of generosity, good will and altruism. Such traits are desirable, but they are also more or less constant expressions of human nature. There is much in the present situation that stimulates them to active operation. They are probably more marked features of American life than of that of any other civilization at any time. Our charity and philanthropy are partly the manifestation of an uneasy conscience. As such a manifestation, they testify to a realization that a régime of industry carried on for private gain does not satisfy the full human nature of even those who profit by it. The impulse and need which the existing economic régime chokes, through preventing its articulated expression, find outlet in actions that acknowledge a social responsibility which the system as a system denies. Hence the development of philanthropic measures is not only compensatory to a stifling of human nature undergone in business, but it is in a way prophetic. Construction is better than relief; prevention than cure. Activities by way of relief of poverty and its attendant mental strains and physical ills—and our philanthropic activities including even the endowment of educational institutions have their ultimate causes in the existence of economic insecurity and distress—suggest, in dim forecast, a society in which daily occupations and relationships will give independence and substantial living to all normal individuals who share in its ongoings, reserving relief for extraordinary emergencies. One does not need to reflect upon the personal motives of great philanthropists to see in what they do an emphatic record of the breakdown of our existing economic organization.

For the chief obstacle to the creation of a type of individual whose pattern of thought and desire is enduringly marked by consensus with others, and in whom sociability is one with coöperation in all regular human associations, is the persistence of that feature of the earlier individualism which defines industry and commerce by ideas of private pecuniary profit. Why, once more, is there such zeal for standardized likeness? It is not, I imagine, because conformity for its own sake appears to be a great boon. It is rather because a certain kind of conformity gives defense and protection to the pecuniary features of our present régime. The foreground may be filled with depiction of the horror of change, and with clamor for law and order and the support of the Constitution. But behind there is desire for perpetuation of that régime which defines individual initiative and ability by success in conducting business so as to make money.

It is not too much to say that the whole significance of the older individualism has now shrunk to a pecuniary scale and measure. The virtues that are supposed to attend rugged individualism may be vocally proclaimed, but it takes no great insight to see that what is cherished is measured by its connection with those activities that make for success in business conducted for personal gain. Hence, the irony of the gospel of "individualism" in business conjoined with suppression of individuality in thought and speech. One cannot imagine a bitterer comment on any professed individualism than that it subordinates the only creative individuality—that of mind—to the maintenance of a régime which gives the few an opportunity for being shrewd in the management of monetary business.

It is claimed, of course, that the individualism of economic self-seeking, even if it has not produced the adjustment of ability and reward and the harmony of interests earlier predicted, has given us the advantage of material prosperity. It is not needful to raise here the question of how far that material prosperity extends. For it is not true that its moving cause is pecuniary individualism. That has been the cause of some great fortunes, but not of national wealth; it counts in the process of distribution, but not in ultimate creation. Scientific insight taking effect in machine technology has been the great productive force. For the most part, economic individualism interpreted as energy and enterprise devoted to private profit, has been an adjunct, often a parasitical one, to the movement of technical and scientific forces.

The scene in which individuality is created has been transformed. The pioneer, such as is depicted in the quotation from Crothers, had no great need for any ideas beyond those that sprang up in the immediate tasks in which he was engaged. His intellectual problems grew out of struggle with the forces of physical nature. The wilderness was a reality and it had to be subdued. The type of character that evolved was strong and hardy, often picturesque, and sometimes heroic. Individuality was a reality because it corresponded to conditions. Irrelevant traditional ideas in religion and morals were carried along, but they were reduced to a size where they did no harm; indeed, they could easily be interpreted in such a way as to be a reinforcement to the sturdy and a consolation to the weak and failing.

But it is no longer a physical wilderness that has to be wrestled with. Our problems grow out of social conditions: they concern human relations rather than man's direct relationship to physical nature. The adventure of the individual, if there is to be any venturing of individuality and not a relapse into the deadness of complacency or of despairing discontent, is an unsubdued social frontier. The issues cannot be met with ideas improvised for the occasion. The problems to be solved are general, not local. They concern complex forces that are at work throughout the whole country, not those limited to an immediate and almost face-to-face environment. Traditional ideas are more than irrelevant. They are an encumbrance; they are the chief obstacle to the formation of a new individuality integrated within itself and with a liberated function in the society wherein it exists. A new individualism can be achieved only through the controlled use of all the resources of the science and technology that have mastered the physical forces of nature.

They are not controlled now in any fundamental sense. Rather do they control us. They are indeed physically controlled. Every factory, power-house and railway system testifies to the fact that we have attained this measure of control. But control of power through the machine is not control of the machine itself. Control of the energies of nature by science is not controlled use of science. We are not even approaching a climax of control; we are hardly at its feeble beginnings. For control is relative to consequences, ends, values; and we do not manage, we hardly have commenced to dream of managing, physical power for the sake of projected purposes and prospective goods. The machine took us unawares and unprepared. Instead of forming new purposes commensurate with its potentialities, we accordingly tried to make it the servant of aims that were the expression of an age when mastery of natural energies on any large scale was the fantasy of magic. As Clarence Ayres has said: "Our industrial revolution began, as some historians say, with half a dozen technical improvements in the textile industry; and it took us a century to realize that anything of moment had happened to us beyond the obvious improvement of spinning and weaving."

I do not say that the aims and values of the earlier day were petty in themselves. But they are almost inconceivably petty in comparison with the means now at our command—if we had an imagination large enough to encompass their potential uses. They are worse than petty; they are confusing and distracting when men are confronted with the physical instrumentalities and agencies which, in the lack of comprehensive purpose and concerted planning, work blindly and carry us drifting hither and yon. I cannot obtain intellectual, moral or esthetic satisfaction from the professed philosophy which animates Bolshevik Russia. But I am sure that the future historian of our times will combine admiration of those who had the imagination first to see that the resources of technology might be directed by organized planning to serve chosen ends with astonishment at the intellectual and moral hebetude of other peoples who were technically so much further advanced.

There is no greater sign of the paralysis of the imagination which custom and involvement in immediate detail can induce than the belief, sedulously propagated by some who pride themselves on superior taste, that the machine is itself the source of our troubles. Of course immense potential resources impose responsibility, and it has yet to be demonstrated whether human capacity can rise to utilization of the opportunities which the machine and technology have opened to us. But it is hard to think of anything more childish than the animism that puts the blame on machinery. For machinery means an undreamed-of reservoir of power. If we have harnessed this power to the dollar rather than to the liberation and enrichment of human life, it is because we have been content to stay within the bounds of traditional aims and values although we are in possession of a revolutionary transforming instrument. Repetition of the older credo of individualism is but the evidence of contentment within these bonds. I for one think it is incredible that this particular form of confession of inferiority will endure very much longer. When we begin to ask what can be done with the machine for the creation and fulfillment of values corresponding to its potency and begin organized planning to effect these goods, a new individual correlative to the realities of the age in which we live will also begin to take form.

Revolt against the machine as the author of social evils usually has an esthetic origin. A more intellectual and quasi-philosophic reaction finds natural science to be their source; or if not science itself (which is allowed to be all very well if it keeps its appropriate humble place) then the attitude of those who depend upon science as an organ of vision and light. Contempt for nature is understandable, at least historically; even though it seems both intellectually petty and morally ungracious to feel contempt for the matrix of our being and the inescapable condition of our lives. But that men should fear and dislike the method of approach to nature I do not find understandable. The eye sees many foul things and the arm and hand do many cruel things. Yet the fanatic who would pluck out the eye and cut off the arm is recognized for what he is. Science, one may say, is but the extension of our natural organs of approach to nature. And I do not mean merely an extension in quantitative range and penetration, as a microscope multiplies the capacity of the unaided eye, but an extension of insight and understanding through bringing relationships and interactions into view. Since we must in any case approach nature in some fashion and by some path—if only that of death—I confess my total inability to understand those who object to an intelligently controlled approach—for that is what science is.

The only way in which I can obtain any sympathetic realization of their attitude is by recalling that there have been those who have professed adoration of science—writing it with a capital S—; those who have thought of it not as a method of approach but as a kind of self-enclosed entity and end in itself, a new theology of self-sufficient authoritatively revealed inherent and absolute Truth. It would, however, seem simpler to correct their misapprehension than first to share it and then to reverse their worship into condemnation. The opposite of intelligent method is no method at all or blind and stupid method. It is a curious state of mind which finds pleasure in setting forth the "limits of science." For the intrinsic limit of knowledge is simply ignorance; and the point in extolling ignorance is not clear except when expressed by those who profit by keeping others in ignorance. There is of course an extrinsic limit of science. But that limitation lies in the ineptitude of those who put it to use; its removal lies in rectification of its use, not in abuse of the thing used.

This reference to science and technology is relevant because they are the forces of present life which are finally significant. It is through employing them with understanding of their possible import that a new individualism, consonant with the realities of the present age, may be brought into operative being. There are many levels and many elements in both the individual and his relations. Neither can be comprehended nor dealt with in mass. Discriminative sensitivity, selection, is imperative. Art is the fruit of such selection when it is given objective effect. The art which our times needs in order to create a new type of individuality is the art which, being sensitive to the technology and science that are the moving forces of our time, will envisage the expansive, the social, culture which they may be made to serve. I am not anxious to depict the form which this emergent individualism will assume. Indeed, I do not see how it can be described until more progress has been made in its production. But such progress will not be initiated until we cease opposing the socially corporate to the individual, and until we develop a constructively imaginative observation of the rôle of science and technology in actual society. The greatest obstacle to that vision is, I repeat, the perpetuation of the older individualism now reduced, as I have said, to the utilization of science and technology for ends of private pecuniary gain. I sometimes wonder if those who are conscious of present ills but who direct their blows of criticism at everything except this obstacle are not stirred by motives which they unconsciously prefer to keep below consciousness.

Chapter VI

CAPITALISTIC OR PUBLIC
SOCIALISM?

I ONCE HEARD a distinguished lawyer say
that the earlier American ideas about individual
initiative and enterprise could be recovered by
an amendment of a few lines to the federal Constitution. The amendment would prohibit all
joint stock enterprises and permit only individual liability to have a legal status. He was, I
think, the only unadulterated Jeffersonian
Democrat I have ever met. He was also logical.
He did not delude himself into supposing that
the pioneer gospel of personal initiative, enterprise, energy and reward could be maintained in
an era of aggregated corporate capital, of mass
production and distribution, of impersonal ownership and of ownership divorced from management. Our political life, however, continues to
ignore the change that has taken place except

as circumstances force it to take account of it in sporadic matters.

The myth is still current that socialism desires to use political means in order to divide wealth equally among all individuals, and that it is consequently opposed to the development of trusts, mergers and consolidated business in general. It is regarded, in other words, as a kind of arithmetically fractionized individualism. This notion of socialism is of the sort that would naturally be entertained by those who cannot get away from the inherent conception of the individual as an isolated and independent unit. In reality, Karl Marx was the prophet of just the period of economic consolidation. If his ghost hovers above the American scene, it must find legitimate satisfaction in our fulfillment of his predictions.

In these predictions, however, Marx reasoned too much from psychological economic premises and depended too little upon technological causes—the application of science to steam, electricity and chemical processes. That is to say, he argued to an undue extent from an alleged constant appropriation by capitalists of all surplus values created by the workers—surplus being

SOCIALISM

defined as anything above the minimum needed for their continued subsistence. He had no conception, moreover, of the capacity of expanding industry to develop new inventions so as to develop new wants, new forms of wealth, new occupations; nor did he imagine that the intellectual ability of the employing class would be equal to seeing the need for sustaining consuming power by high wages in order to keep up production and its profits. This explains why his prediction of a revolution in political control, caused by the general misery of the masses and resulting in the establishment of a socialistic society, has not been realized in this country. Nevertheless, the issue which he raised—the relation of the economic structure to political operations—is one that actively persists.

Indeed, it forms the only basis of present political questions. An intelligent and experienced observer of affairs at Washington has said that all political questions which he has heard discussed in Washington come back ultimately to problems connected with the distribution of income. Wealth, property and the processes of manufacturing and distribution—down to retail trade through the chain system—can hardly be socialized in outward effect without a political repercussion. It constitutes an ultimate issue which must be faced by new or existing political parties. There is still enough vitality in the older individualism to offer a very serious handicap to any party or program which calls itself by the name of Socialism. But in the long run, the realities of the situation will exercise control over the connotations which, for historical reasons, cling to a word. In view of this fact, the fortunes of a party called by a given name are insignificant.

In one important sense, the fundamental character of the economic question is not ignored in present politics. The dominant party has officially constituted itself the guardian of prosperity; it has gone further and offered itself as the author of prosperity. It has insinuated itself in that guise into the imagination of a sufficient number of citizens and voters so that it owes its continuing denomination to its identification with prosperity. Our presidential elections are upon the whole determined by fear. Hundreds of thousands of citizens who vote independently or for Democratic candidates at local elections and in off-year congressional elections regularly vote the Republican ticket every four years. They do so because of a vague but influential dread lest a monkey-wrench be thrown into the economic and financial machine. The dread is as general among the workers as among small traders and storekeepers. It is basically the asset that keeps the dominant party in office. Our whole industrial scheme is so complex, so delicately interdependent in its varied parts, so responsive to a multitude of subtle influences, that it seems definitely better to the mass of voters to endure the ills they may already suffer rather than take the chance of disturbing industry. Even in the election of 1928, in spite of both the liquor and the Catholic issue, this was, I believe the determining factor.

Moreover, the fact that Hoover offered himself to the popular imagination as a man possessed of the engineer's rather than the politician's mind was a great force. Engineering has accomplished great things; its triumphs are everywhere in evidence. The miracles that it has wrought have given it the prestige of magical wonder-working. A people sick of politicians felt in some half-conscious way that the mind, experience, and gifts of an engineer would bring healing and order into our political life. It is impossible to present statistics as to the exact force of the factors mentioned. Judgment on the two points, especially the latter, must remain a matter of opinion. But the identification of the Republican party with the maintenance of prosperity cannot be denied, and the desire for the engineer in politics is general enough to be at least symptomatic.

Prosperity is largely a state of mind, and belief in it is even more so. It follows that skepticism about its extent is of little importance when the mental tide runs with the idea. Although figures can be quoted to show how spotty it is, and how inequitably its economic conditions are distributed, they are all to no avail. What difference does it make that eleven thousand people, having each an annual income of over $100,000, appropriated in 1927 about one-twenty-fifth of the net national income? What good does it do to cite official figures showing that only twenty per cent of the income of the favored eleven thousand came from salaries and from profits of the businesses they were personally engaged in, while the remaining eighty per cent was derived from investments, speculative profits, rent, etc.? That the total earnings of eight million wage workers should be only four times the amount of what the income-tax returns frankly call the "unearned" income of the eleven thousand millionaires goes almost without notice. Moreover, income from investments in corporate aggregations increases at the expense of that coming from enterprises personally managed. For anyone to call attention to this discrepancy is considered an aspersion on our rugged individualism and an attempt to stir up class feeling. Meanwhile, the income-tax returns for 1928 show that in seven years the number of persons having an annual income of more than $1,000,-000 has increased from sixty-seven to almost five hundred, twenty-four of whom had incomes of over $10,000,000 each.

Nevertheless, the assumption of guardianship of prosperity by a political party means the assumption of responsibility, and in the long run the ruling economic-political combination will be held to account. The overlords will have to do something to make good. This fact seems to me to be the center of the future political situation. Discussion of the prospective political development in connection with corporate industry may at least start from the fact that the industries which used to be regarded as staple, as the foundations of sound economy, are depressed. The plight of agriculture, of the coal and textile industries, is well known. The era of great railway expansion has come to a close; the building trades have a fluctuating career. The counterpart of this fact is that the now flourishing industries are those connected with and derived from new technical developments. Without the rapid growth in the manufacture and sale of automobiles, radios, airplanes, etc.; without the rapid development of new uses for electricity and super-power, prosperity in the last few years would hardly have been even a state of mind. Economic stimulus has come largely from these new uses for capital and labor; surplus funds drawn from them have kept the stock market and other forms of business actively going. At the same time, these newer developments have accelerated the accumulation and concentration of super-fortunes.

These facts seem to suggest the issue of future politics. The fact of depression has already influenced political action in legislation and administration. What will happen when industries now new become in turn overcapitalized, and consumption does not keep up in proportion to investment in them; when they, too, have an excess capacity of production? There are now, it is estimated, eight billions of surplus savings a year, and the amount is increasing. Where is this capital to find its outlet? Diversion into the stock market gives temporary relief, but the resulting inflation is a "cure" which creates a new disease. If it goes into the expansion of industrial plants, how long will it be before they, too, "overproduce"? The future seems to hold in store an extension of political control in the social interest. We already have the Interstate Commerce Commission, the Federal Reserve Board, and now the Farm Relief Board—a socialistic undertaking on a large scale sponsored by the party of individualism. The probabilities seem to favor the creation of more such boards in the future, in spite of all concomitant denunciations of bureaucracy and proclamations that individualism is the source of our national prosperity.

The tariff question, too, is undergoing a change. Now, it is the older industries which, being depressed, clamor for relief. The "infant" industries are those which are indifferent, and which, with their growing interest in export trade, are likely to become increasingly indifferent or hostile. The alignment of political parties has not indeed been affected so far by economic changes—beyond the formation of insurgent blocs within the old parties. But this fact only conceals from view the greater fact that, under cover of the old parties, legislation and administration have taken on new functions due to the impact of trade and finance. The most striking example, of course, is the effort to use governmental agencies and large public funds to put agriculture on a parity with other forms of industry. The case is the more significant because the farmers form the part of the population that has remained most faithful to the old individualistic philosophy, and because the movement is definitely directed to bringing them within the scope of collective and corporate action. The policy of using public works to alleviate unemployment in times of depression is another, if lesser, sign of the direction which political action is taking.

The question of whether and how far the newer industries will follow the cycle of the older and now depressed ones, becoming overcapitalized, overproductive in capacity and overcharged with carrying costs, is, of course, a speculative one. The negative side of the argument demands, however, considerable optimism. It is at least reasonably certain that if depression sets in with them, the process of public intervention and public control will be repeated. And in any case, nothing can permanently exclude political action with reference to old age and unemployment. The scandalous absence even of public inquiry and statistics is emphasized at present by the displacement of workers through technical developments, and by the lowering, because of speeded-up processes, of the age-limit at which workers can be profitably employed. Unemployment, on the scale at which it now "normally" exists—to say nothing of its extent during cyclic periods of depression—is a confession of the breakdown of unregulated individualistic industry conducted for private profit. Coal miners and even farmers may go unheeded, but not so the industrial city workers. One of the first signs of the reawakening of an aggressive labor movement will be the raising of the unemployment problem to a political issue. The outcome of this will be a further extension of public control.

Political prophecy is a risky affair and I would not venture into details. But large and basic economic currents cannot be ignored for any great length of time, and they are working in one direction. There are many indications that the reactionary tendencies which have controlled American politics are coming to a term. The inequitable distribution of income will bring to the fore the use of taxing power to effect redistribution by means of larger taxation of swollen income and by heavier death duties on large fortunes. The scandal of private appropriation of socially produced values in unused land cannot forever remain unconcealed. The situation in world production and commerce is giving "protection and free trade" totally new meanings.

The connection of municipal mismanagement and corruption with special favors to big economic interests, and the connection of the alliance thus formed with crime, are becoming more generally recognized. Local labor bodies are getting more and more discontented with the policy of political abstention and with the farce of working through parties controlled by adverse interests. The movement is cumulative and includes convergence to a common head of many now isolated factors. When a focus is reached, economic issues will be openly and not merely covertly political. The problem of social control of industry and the use of governmental agencies for constructive social ends will become the avowed center of political struggle.

A chapter is devoted to the political phase of the situation not because it is supposed the place of definitely political action in the resolution of the present split in life is fundamental. But it is accessory. A certain amount of specific change in legislation and administration is required in order to supply the conditions under which other changes may take place in nonpolitical ways. Moreover, the psychological effect of law and political discussion is enormous. Political action provides large-scale models that react into the formation of ideas and ideals about all social matters. One sure way in which the individual who is politically lost, because of the loss of objects to which his loyalties can attach themselves, could recover a composed mind, would be by apprehension of the realities of industry and finance as they function in public and political life. Political apathy such as has marked our thought for many years past is due fundamentally to mental confusion arising from lack of consciousness of any vital connection between politics and daily affairs. The parties have been eager accomplices in maintaining the confusion and unreality. To know where things are going and why they are is to have the material out of which stable objects of purpose and loyalty may be formed. To perceive clearly the actual movement of events is to be on the road to intellectual clarity and order.

The chief value of political reference is that politics so well exemplify the existing social confusion and its causes. The various expressions of public control to which reference has been made have taken place sporadically and in response

to the pressure of distressed groups so large
that their voting power demanded attention.
They have been improvised to meet special occasions. They have not been adopted as parts of
any general social policy. Consequently their real
import has not been considered; they have been
treated as episodic exceptions. We live politically
from hand to mouth. Corporate forces are strong
enough to secure attention and action now and
then, when some emergency forces them upon us,
but acknowledgment of them does not inspire
consecutive policy. On the other hand, the older
individualism is still sufficiently ingrained to obtain allegiance in confused sentiment and in vo-
cal utterance. It persists to such an extent that
we can maintain the illusion that it regulates our
political thought and behavior. In actuality, appeal to it serves to perpetuate the current disor-
ganization in which financial and industrial
power, corporately organized, can deflect economic consequences away from the advantage of
the many to serve the privilege of the few.

I know of no recent event so politically interesting as President Hoover's calling of industrial
conferences after the stock-market crash of 1929.

INDIVIDUALISM—OLD AND NEW

It is indicative of many things, some of them actual, some of them dimly and ambiguously possible. It testifies to the disturbance created when the prospect of an industrial depression faces a party and administration that have assumed responsibility for prosperity through having claimed credit for it. It testifies to the import of the crowd psychology of suggestion and credulity in American life. Christian Science rules American thought in business affairs; if we can be led to think that certain things do not exist, they perforce have not happened. These conferences also give evidence of our national habit of planlessness in social affairs, of locking the barn door after the horse has been stolen. For nothing was done until after a crash which every economist—except those hopelessly committed to the doctrine of a "new economic era"—knew was certain to happen, however uncertain they may have been as to its time.

The more ambiguous meaning of these conferences is connected with future developments. It is clear that one of their functions was to add up columns of figures to imposing totals, with a view to their effect on the public imagination. Will there be more than a psychological and arithmetical outcome? A hopeful soul may take it as the beginning of a real application of the engineering mind to social life in its economic phase. He may persuade himself that it is the commencement of the acceptance of social responsibility on a large scale by American industrialists, financiers and politicians. He may envisage a permanent Economic Council finally growing out of the holding of a series of conferences, a council which shall take upon itself a planned coördination of industrial development. He may be optimistic enough to anticipate a time when representatives of labor will meet on equal terms, not for the sake of obtaining a pledge to abstain from efforts to obtain a rise of wages and from strikes, but as an integral factor in maintaining a planned regulation of the bases of national welfare.

The issue is still in the future and uncertain. What is not uncertain is that any such move would, if carried through, mark the acknowledged end of the old social and political epoch and its dominant philosophy. It would be in accord with the spirit of American life if the movement were undertaken by voluntary agreement and endeavor rather than by governmental coercion. There is that much enduring truth in our individualism. But the outcome would surely involve the introduction of social responsibility into our business system to such an extent that the doom of an exclusively pecuniary-profit industry would follow. A coördinating and directive council in which captains of industry and finance would meet with representatives of labor and public officials to plan the regulation of industrial activity would signify that we had entered constructively and voluntarily upon the road which Soviet Russia is traveling with so much attendant destruction and coercion. While, as I have already said, political action is not basic, concentration of attention upon real and vital issues such as attend the public control of industry and finance for the sake of social values would have vast intellectual and emotional reverberations. No phase of our culture would remain unaffected. Politics is a means, not an end. But thought of it as a means will lead to thought of the ends it should serve. It will induce consideration of the ways in which a worthy and rich life for all may be achieved. In so doing, it will restore directive aims and be a significant step forward in the recovery of a unified individuality.

I have tried to make a brief survey of the possibilities of the political situation in general, and not to make either a plea or a prophecy of special political alignments. But any kind of political regeneration within or without the present parties demands first of all a frank intellectual recognition of present tendencies. In a society so rapidly becoming corporate, there is need of associated thought to take account of the realities of the situation and to frame policies in the social interest. Only then can organized action in behalf of the social interest be made a reality. We are in for some kind of socialism, call it by whatever name we please, and no matter what it will be called when it is realized. Economic determinism is now a fact, not a theory. But there is a difference and a choice between a blind, chaotic and unplanned determinism, issuing from business conducted for pecuniary profit, and the deter-

INDIVIDUALISM—OLD AND NEW

mination of a socially planned and ordered development. It is the difference and the choice between a socialism that is public and one that is capitalistic.

Chapter VII

THE CRISIS IN CULTURE

Discussion of the state and prospects of American culture abounds. But "culture" is an ambiguous word. With respect to one of its meanings I see no ground for pessimism. Interest in art, science and philosophy is not on the wane; the contrary is the case. There may have been individuals superior in achievement in the past; but I do not know of any time in our history when so many persons were actively concerned, both as producers and as appreciators, with these culminating aspects of civilization. There is a more lively and more widespread interest in ideas, in critical discussion, in all that forms an intellectual life, than ever before. Anyone who can look back over a span of thirty or forty years must be conscious of the difference that a generation has produced. And the movement is going forward, not backward.

About culture in the sense of cultivation of a number of persons, a number on the increase rather than the decrease, I find no ground for any great solicitude. But "culture" has another meaning. It denotes the type of emotion and thought that is characteristic of a people and epoch as a whole, an organic intellectual and moral quality. Without raising the ambiguous question of aristocracy, one can say without fear of denial that a high degree of personal cultivation at the top of society can coexist with a low and unworthy state of culture as a pervasive manifestation of social life. The marvelous achievement of the novel, music and the drama in the Russia of the Czar's day sufficiently illustrates what is meant. Nor is preoccupation with commerce and wealth an insuperable bar to a flourishing culture. One may cite the fact that the highest phase of Dutch painting came in a time of just such expansion. And so it was with the Periclean, Augustan and Elizabethan ages. Excellence of personal cultivation has often, and perhaps usually, been coincident with the political and economic dominance of a few and with periods of material expansion.

THE CRISIS IN CULTURE

I see no reason why we in the United States should not also have golden ages of literature and science. But we are given to looking at this and that "age" marked with great names and great productivity, while forgetting to ask about the roots of the efflorescence. Might it not be argued that the very transitoriness of the glory of these ages proves that its causes were sporadic and accidental? And in any case, a question must be raised as to the growth of native culture in our own country. The idea of democracy is doubtless as ambiguous as is that of aristocracy. But we cannot evade a basic issue. Unless an avowedly democratic people and an undeniably industrial time can achieve something more than an "age" of high personal cultivation, there is something deeply defective in its culture. Such an age would be American in a topographical sense, not in a spiritual one.

This fact gives significance to the question so often raised as to whether the material and mechanistic forces of the machine age are to crush the higher life. In one sense I find, as I have already said, no special danger. Poets, painters, novelists, dramatists, philosophers, scientists, are sure to appear and to find an appreciative audience. But the unique fact about our own civilization is that if it is to achieve and manifest a characteristic culture, it must develop, not on top of an industrial and political substructure, but out of our material civilization itself. It will come by turning a machine age into a significantly new habit of mind and sentiment, or it will not come at all. A cultivation of a class that externally adorns a material civilization will at most merely repeat the sort of thing that has transiently happened many times before.

The question, then, is not merely a quantitative one. It is not a matter of an increased number of persons who will take part in the creation and enjoyment of art and science. It is a qualitative question. Can a material, industrial civilization be converted into a distinctive agency for liberating the minds and refining the emotions of all who take part in it? The cultural question is a political and economic one before it is a definitely cultural one.

It is a commonplace that the problem of the relation of mechanistic and industrial civilization to culture is the deepest and most urgent problem of our day. If interpreters are correct in saying that "Americanization" is becoming universal, it is a problem of the world and not just of our own country—although it is first acutely experienced here. It raises issues of the widest philosophic import. The question of the relation of man and nature, of mind and matter, assumes its vital significance in this context. A "humanism" that separates man from nature will envisage a radically different solution of the industrial and economic perplexities of the age than the humanism entertained by those who find no uncrossable gulf or fixed gap. The former will inevitably look backward for direction; it will strive for a cultivated élite supported on the backs of toiling masses. The latter will have to face the question of whether work itself can become an instrument of culture and of how the masses can share freely in a life enriched in imagination and esthetic enjoyment. This task is set not because of sentimental "humanitarianism," but as the necessary conclusion of the intellectual conviction that while man belongs in nature and mind is connected with matter, humanity and its collective intelligence are the means by which nature is guided to new possibilities.

Many European critics openly judge American life from the standpoint of a dualism of the spiritual and material, and deplore the primacy of the physical as fatal to any culture. They fail to see the depth and range of our problem, which is that of making the material an active instrument in the creation of the life of ideas and art. Many American critics of the present scene are engaged in devising modes of escape. Some flee to Paris or Florence; others take flight in their imagination to India, Athens, the middle ages or the American age of Emerson, Thoreau and Melville. Flight is solution by evasion. Return to a dualism consisting of a massive substratum of the material upon which are erected spiritually ornamented façades is flatly impossible, except upon the penalty of the spiritual disenfranchisement of those permanently condemned to toil mechanically at the machine.

That the cultural problem must be reached through economic roads is testified to by our educational system. No nation has ever been so actively committed to universal schooling as are the people of the United States. But what is our system for? What ends does it serve? That it gives opportunity to many who would otherwise lack it is undeniable. It is also the agency of important welding and fusing processes. These are conditions of creation of a mind that will constitute a distinctive type of culture. But they are conditions only. If our public-school system merely turns out efficient industrial fodder and citizenship fodder in a state controlled by pecuniary industry, as other schools in other nations have turned out efficient cannon fodder, it is not helping to solve the problem of building up a distinctive American culture; it is only aggravating the problem. That which prevents the schools from doing their educational work freely is precisely the pressure—for the most part indirect, to be sure—of domination by the money-motif of our economic régime. The subject is too large to deal with here. But the distinguishing trait of the American student body in our higher schools is a kind of intellectual immaturity. This immaturity is mainly due to their enforced mental seclusion; there is, in their schooling, little free and disinterested concern with the underlying social problems of our civilization. Other typical evidence is found in the training of engineers. Thorstein Veblen—and many others have since repeated his idea—pointed out the strategic position occupied by the engineer in our industrial and technological activity. Engineering schools give excellent technical training. Where is the school that pays systematic attention to the potential social function of the engineering profession?

I refer to the schools in connection with this problem of American culture because they are the formal agencies for producing those mental attitudes, those modes of feeling and thinking, which are the essence of a distinctive culture. But they are not the ultimate formative force. Social institutions, the trend of occupations, the pattern of social arrangements, are the finally controlling influences in shaping minds. The immaturity nurtured in schools is carried over into life. If we Americans manifest, as compared with those of other countries who have had the benefits of higher schooling, a kind of infantilism, it is because our own schooling so largely evades serious consideration of the deeper issues of social life;

for it is only through induction into realities that mind can be matured. Consequently the effective education, that which really leaves a stamp on character and thought, is obtained when graduates come to take their part in the activities of an adult society which put exaggerated emphasis upon business and the results of business success. Such an education is at best extremely one-sided; it operates to create the specialized "business mind" and this, in turn, is manifested in leisure as well as in business itself. The one-sidedness is accentuated because of the tragic irrelevancy of prior schooling to the controlling realities of social life. There is little preparation to induce either hardy resistance, discriminating criticism, or the vision and desire to direct economic forces in new channels.

If, then, I select education for special notice, it is because education—in the broad sense of formation of fundamental attitudes of imagination, desire and thinking—is strictly correlative with culture in its inclusive social sense. It is because the educative influence of economic and political institutions is, in the last analysis, even more important than their immediate economic

INDIVIDUALISM—OLD AND NEW

consequences. The mental poverty that comes from one-sided distortion of mind is ultimately more significant than poverty in material goods. To make this assertion is not to gloss over the material harshness that exists. It is rather to point out that under present conditions these material results cannot be separated from development of mind and character. Destitution on the one side and wealth on the other are factors in the determination of that psychological and moral constitution which is the source and the measure of attained culture. I can think of nothing more childishly futile, for example, than the attempt to bring "art" and esthetic enjoyment externally to the multitudes who work in the ugliest surroundings and who leave their ugly factories only to go through depressing streets to eat, sleep and carry on their domestic occupations in grimy, sordid homes. The interest of the younger generation in art and esthetic matters is a hopeful sign of the growth of culture in its narrower sense. But it will readily turn into an escape mechanism unless it develops into an alert interest in the conditions which determine the esthetic environment of the vast mul-

THE CRISIS IN CULTURE

titudes who now live, work and play in surroundings that perforce degrade their tastes and that unconsciously educate them into desire for any kind of enjoyment as long as it is cheap and "exciting."

It is the work of sociologists, psychologists, novelists, dramatists and poets to exhibit the consequences of our present economic régime upon taste, desire, satisfaction and standards of value. An article like this cannot do a work which requires many volumes. But a paragraph suffices to call attention to one central fact. Most of those who are engaged in the outward work of production and distribution of economic commodities have no share—imaginative, intellectual, emotional—in directing the activities in which they physically participate.

It was remarked in an earlier chapter that there is definite restriction placed upon existing corporateness. It is found in the fact that economic associations are fixed in ways which exclude most of the workers in them from taking part in their management. The subordination of the enterprises to pecuniary profit reacts to make

131

the workers "hands" only. Their hearts and brains are not engaged. They execute plans which they do not form, and of whose meaning and intent they are ignorant—beyond the fact that these plans make a profit for others and secure a wage for themselves. To set forth the consequences of this fact upon the experience and the minds of uncounted multitudes would again require volumes. But there is an undeniable limitation of opportunities; and minds are warped, frustrated, unnourished by their activities—the ultimate source of all constant nurture of the spirit. The philosopher's idea of a complete separation of mind and body is realized in thousands of industrial workers, and the result is a depressed body and an empty and distorted mind.

There are instances, here and there, of the intellectual and moral effects which accrue when workers can employ their feelings and imaginations as well as their muscles in what they do. But it is still impossible to foresee in detail what would happen if a system of coöperative control of industry were generally substituted for the present system of exclusion. There would be an enormous liberation of mind, and the mind thus set free would have constant direction and nourishment. Desire for related knowledge, physical and social, would be created and rewarded; initiative and responsibility would be demanded and achieved. One may not, perhaps, be entitled to predict that an efflorescence of a distinctive social culture would immediately result. But one can say without hesitation that we shall attain only the personal cultivation of a class, and not a characteristic American culture, unless this condition is fulfilled. It is impossible for a highly industrialized society to attain a widespread high excellence of mind when multitudes are excluded from occasion for the use of thought and emotion in their daily occupations. The contradiction is so great and so pervasive that a favorable issue is hopeless. We must wrest our general culture from an industrialized civilization; and this fact signifies that industry must itself become a primary educative and cultural force for those engaged in it. The conception that natural science somehow sets a limit to freedom, subjecting men to fixed necessities, is not an intrinsic product of science. Just as with the popular notion that art is a luxury, whose proper abode is the museum and gallery, the notion of literary persons (including some philosophers) that science is an oppression due to the material structure of nature, is ultimately a reflex of the social conditions under which science is applied so as to reach only a pecuniary fruition. Knowledge takes effect in machinery and in the minds of technical directors, but not in the thoughts of those who tend the machines. The alleged fatalism of science is in reality the fatalism of the pecuniary order in which science is employed.

If I have emphasized the effect upon the wage workers, it is not because the consequences are not equally marked with respect to the few who now enjoy the material emoluments of the system and monopolize its management and control. There will doubtless always be leaders, those who will have the more active and leading share in the intellectual direction of great industrial undertakings. But as long as the direction is more concerned with pecuniary profit than with social utility, the resulting intellectual and moral development will be one-sided and warped. An inevitable result of a coöperatively shared con-

THE CRISIS IN CULTURE

trol of industry would be the recognition of final use or consumption as the criterion of valuation, decision and direction. When the point of view of consumption is supreme in industry, the latter will be socialized, and I see no way of securing its genuine socialization save as industry is viewed and conducted from the standpoint of the user and enjoyer of services and commodities. For then human values will control economic values. Moreover, as long as means are kept separate from human ends (the consequences produced in human living), "values in use" will be so dominated by exchange or sale values that the former will be interpreted by means of the latter. In other words, there is now no inherent criterion for consumption-values. "Wealth," as Ruskin so vehemently pointed out, includes as much *illth* as well-being. When values in use are the ends of industry they will receive a scrutiny and criticism for which there is no foundation at present, save external moralizing and exhortation. Production for private profit signifies that any kind of consumption will be stimulated that leads to private gain.

There can be no stable and balanced development of mind and character apart from the assumption of responsibility. In an industrialized society, that responsibility must for the most part be associated with industry, since it will grow indirectly out of industry even for those not engaged in it. The wider and fuller the sense of social consequences—that is, of the effect on the life-experience of the consumer—the deeper and surer, the more stable, is the intelligence of those who have the foremost place in the direction of industry. A society saturated with industrialism may evolve a class of highly cultivated persons in the traditional sense of cultivation. But there will be something thin and meager about even this meed of cultivation if it evolves in isolation from the main currents of action in which thought and desire are engaged. As long as imagination is concerned primarily with obtaining pecuniary success and enjoying its material results, the type of culture will conform to these standards.

Everywhere and at all times the development of mind and its cultural products have been connate with the channels in which mind is exercised and applied. This fact defines the problem of creating a culture that will be characteristically our own. Escape from industrialism on the ground that it is unesthetic and brutal can win only a superficial and restricted success of esteem. It is a silly caricature to interpret such statements as meaning that science should devote itself directly to solving industrial problems, or that poetry and painting should find their material in machines and in machine processes. The question is not one of idealizing present conditions in esthetic treatment, but of discovering and trying to realize the conditions under which vital esthetic production and esthetic appreciation may take place on a generous social scale.

And similarly for science; it is not in the least a matter of considering this and that particular practical application to be squeezed out of science: we have a great deal of that sort of thing already. It is a question of acknowledgment on the part of scientific inquirers of intellectual responsibility; of admitting into their consciousness a perception of what science has actually done, through its counterpart technologies, in making the world and life what they are. This perception would bear fruit by raising the question of what science can do in making a different sort of world and society. Such a science would be at the opposite pole to science conceived as merely a means to special industrial ends. It would, indeed, include in its scope all the technological aspects of the latter, but it would also be concerned with control of their social effects. A humane society would use scientific method, and intelligence with its best equipment, to bring about human consequences. Such a society would meet the demand for a science that is humanistic, and not just physical and technical. "Solutions" of the problem of the relation of the material and the spiritual, of the ideal and the actual, are merely conceptual and at best prophetic unless material conditions are idealized by contributing to cultural consequences. Science is a potential tool of such a liberating spiritualization; the arts, including that of social control, are its fruition.

I do not hold, I think, an exaggerated opinion of the influence that is wielded by so-called "intellectuals"—philosophers, professional and otherwise, critics, writers and professional persons in general having interests beyond their immediate callings. But their present position is not a measure of their possibilities. For they are now intellectually dispersed and divided; this fact is one aspect of what I have called "the lost individual." This internal dissolution is necessarily accompanied by a weak social efficacy. The chaos is due, more than to anything else, to mental withdrawal, to the failure to face the realities of industrialized society. Whether the ultimate influence of the distinctively intellectual or reflective groups is to be great or small, an initial move is theirs. A consciously directed critical consideration of the state of present society in its causes and consequences is a pre-condition of projection of constructive ideas. To be effective, the movement must be organized. But this requirement does not demand the creation of a formal organization; it does demand that a sense of the need and opportunity should possess a sufficiently large number of minds. If it does, the results of their inquiries will converge to a common issue.

This point of view is sometimes represented as a virtual appeal to those primarily engaged in inquiry and reflection to desert their studies, libra-

ries, and laboratories and engage in works of
social reform. That representation is a caricature. It is not the abandonment of thinking and
inquiry that is asked for, but more thinking and
more significant inquiry. This "more" is equivalent to a conscious direction of thought and inquiry, and direction can be had only by a realization of problems in the rank of their urgency.
The "clerk" and secretary once occupied, if we
may trust history, places of great influence if
not of honor. In a society of military and political leaders who were illiterate, they must have
done much of the thinking and negotiating for
which the names of the great now receive credit.
The intellectuals of the present are their de-
scendants. Outwardly they have been emanci-
pated and have an independent position formerly
lacking. Whether their actual efficacy has been
correspondingly increased may be doubted. In
some degree, they have attained their liberty in
direct ratio to their distance from the scenes of
action. A more intimate connection would not
signify, I repeat, a surrender of the business of
thought, even speculative thought, for the sake
of getting busy at some so-called practical mat-

ter. Rather would it signify a focussing of thought and intensifying of its quality by bringing it into relation with issues of stupendous meaning.

I am suspicious of all attempts to erect a hierarchy of values: their results generally prove to be inapplicable and abstract. But there is at every time a hierarchy of problems, for there are some issues which underlie and condition others. No one person is going to evolve a constructive solution for the problem of humanizing industrial civilization, of making it and its technology a servant of human life—a problem which is once more equivalent, for us, to that of creating a genuine culture. But general guidance of serious intellectual endeavor by a consciousness of the problem would enable at least one group of individuals to recover a social function and so re-find themselves. And recovery by those with special intellectual gifts and equipment from their enforced social defection is at least a first step in a more general reconstruction that will bring integration out of disorder.

Accordingly, I do not wish my remarks about escape and withdrawal to be interpreted as if they were directed at any special group of persons. The flight of particular individuals is symptomatic of the seclusion of existing science, intelligence and art. The personal gap which, generally speaking, isolates the intellectual worker from the wage earner is symbolic and typical of a deep division of functions. This division is the split between theory and practice in actual operation. The effects of the split are as fatal to culture on the one side as on the other. It signifies that what we call our culture will continue to be, and in increased measure, a survival of inherited European traditions, and that it will not be indigenous. And if it is true, as some hold, that with the extension of machine technology and industrialism the whole world is becoming "Americanized," then the creation of an indigenous culture is no disservice to the traditional European springs of our spiritual life. It will signify, not ingratitude, but the effort to repay a debt.

The solution of the crisis in culture is identical with the recovery of composed, effective and creative individuality. The harmony of individual mind with the realities of a civilization made outwardly corporate by an industry based on technology does not signify that individual minds will be passively molded by existing social conditions as if the latter were fixed and static. When the patterns that form individuality of thought and desire are in line with actuating social forces, that individuality will be released for creative effort. Originality and uniqueness are not opposed to social nurture; they are saved by it from eccentricity and escape. The positive and constructive energy of individuals, as manifested in the remaking and redirection of social forces and conditions, is itself a social necessity. A new culture expressing the possibilities immanent in a machine and material civilization will release whatever is distinctive and potentially creative in individuals, and individuals thus freed will be the constant makers of a continuously new society.

It was said in an earlier chapter that "acceptance" of conditions has two very different meanings. To this statement may now be added the consideration that "conditions" are always moving; they are always in transition to something else. The important question is whether intelligence, whether observation and reflection, intervenes and becomes a directive factor in the transition. The moment it does intervene, conditions become conditions of forecasting consequences; when these consequences present themselves in thought, preference and volition, planning and determination, come into play. To foresee consequences of existing conditions is to surrender neutrality and drift; it is to take sides in behalf of the consequences that are preferred. The cultural consequences that our industrial system now produces have no finality about them. When they are observed and are related discriminatingly to their causes, they become conditions for planning, desiring, choosing. Discriminating inquiry will disclose what part of present results is the outcome of the technological factors at work and what part is due to a legal and economic system which it is within the power of man to modify and transform. It is indeed foolish to assume that an industrial civilization will somehow automatically, from its own inner impetus, produce a new culture. But it is a lazy abdication of responsibility which assumes that a genuine culture can be achieved except first by an active and alert intellectual recognition of the realities of an industrial age, and then by planning to use them in behalf of a significantly human life. To charge that those who urge intellectual acknowledgment or acceptance as the first necessary step stop at this point, and thus end with an optimistic rationalization of the present as if it were final, is a misconstruction that indicates a desire to shirk responsibility for undertaking the task of reconstruction and direction. Or else it waits upon a miracle to beget the culture which is desired by all serious minds.

Chapter VIII

INDIVIDUALITY IN OUR DAY

In the foregoing chapters, I have attempted to portray the split between the idea of the individual inherited from the past and the realities of a situation that is becoming increasingly corporate. Some of the effects produced on living individuality by this division have been indicated. I have urged that individuality will again become integral and vital when it creates a frame for itself by attention to the scene in which it must perforce exist and develop. It is likely that many persons will regard my statement of the problem as a commonplace. Others will deplore my failure to offer a detailed solution and a definite picture of just what an individual would be if he were in harmony with the realities of American civilization. Still others will think that a disease has been described as a remedy; that the articles are an indiscriminate praise of technological science and of a corporate industrial civilization; that they are an effort to boost upon the bandwagon those reluctant to climb.

I have indeed attempted analysis, rather than either a condemnation of the evils of present society or a recommendation of fixed ends and ideals for their cure. For I think that serious minds are pretty well agreed as to both evils and ideals—as long as both are taken in general terms. Condemnation is too often only a way of displaying superiority; it speaks from outside the scene; it discloses symptoms but not causes. It is impotent to produce; it can only reproduce its own kind. As for ideals, all agree that we want the good life, and that the good life involves freedom and a taste that is trained to appreciate the honorable, the true and the beautiful. But as long as we limit ourselves to generalities, the phrases that express ideals may be transferred from conservative to radical or vice versa, and nobody will be the wiser. For, without analysis, they do not descend into the actual scene nor concern themselves with the generative conditions of realization of ideals.

There is danger in the reiteration of eternal

verities and ultimate spiritualities. Our sense of the actual is dulled, and we are led to think that in dwelling upon ideal goals we have somehow transcended existing evils. Ideals express possibilities; but they are genuine ideals only in so far as they are possibilities of what is now moving. Imagination can set them free from their encumbrances and project them as a guide in attention to what now exists. But, save as they are related to actualities, they are pictures in a dream.

I have, then, ventured to suppose that analysis of present conditions is of primary importance. Analysis of even a casual kind discloses that these conditions are not fixed. To accept them intellectually is to perceive that they are in flux. Their movement is not destined to a single end. Many outcomes may be projected, and the movement may be directed by many courses to many chosen goals, once conditions have been recognized for what they are. By becoming conscious of their movements and by active participation in their currents, we may guide them to some preferred possibility. In this interaction, individuals attain an integrated being. The individual who intelligently and actively partakes in a per-

ception that is a first step in conscious choice is
never so isolated as to be lost nor so quiescent
as to be suppressed.

One of the main difficulties in understanding
the present and apprehending its human possibilities is the persistence of stereotypes of spiritual life which were formed in old and alien
cultures. In static societies—those which the industrial revolution has doomed—acquiescence
had a meaning, and so had the projection of fixed
ideals. Things were so relatively settled that
there was something to acquiesce in, and goals
and ideals could be imagined that were as fixed in
their way as existing conditions in theirs. The
medieval legal system could define "just" prices
and wages, for the definition was a formulation
of what was customary in the local community;
it operated merely to prevent exorbitant deviations. It could prescribe a system of definite duties for all relations, for there was a hierarchical
order, and occasions for the exercise of duty fell
within an established and hence known order.
Communities were local; they did not merge,
overlap and interact in all kinds of subtle and

hidden ways. A common church was the guardian and administrator of spiritual and ideal truth, and its theoretical authority had direct channels for making itself felt in the practical details of life. Spiritual realities might have their locus in the next world, but this after-world was intimately tied into all the affairs of this world by an institution existing here and now.

To-day there are no patterns sufficiently enduring to provide anything stable in which to acquiesce, and there is no material out of which to frame final and all-inclusive ends. There is, on the other hand, such constant change that acquiescence is but a series of interrupted spasms, and the outcome is mere drifting. In such a situation, fixed and comprehensive goals are but irrelevant dreams, while acquiescence is not a policy but its abnegation.

Again, the machine is condemned wholesale because it is seen through the eyes of a spirituality that belonged to another state of culture. Present evil consequences are treated as if they were eternally necessary, because they cannot be made consistent with the ideals of another age. In reality, a machine age is a challenge to generate new conceptions of the ideal and the spiritual. Ferrero has said that machines "are the barbarians of modern times, which have destroyed the fairest works of ancient civilization." But even the barbarians were not immutably barbarous; they, too, were bearers of directive movement, and in time they wrought out a civilization that had its own measure of fairness and beauty.

Most attacks on the mechanistic character of science are caused by the survival of philosophies and religions formed when nature was the grim foe of man. The possibility of the present, and therefore its problem, is that through and by science, nature may become the friend and ally of man. I have rarely seen an attack on science as hostile to humanism which did not rest upon a conception of nature formed long before there was any science. That there is much at any time in environing nature which is indifferent and hostile to human values is obvious to any serious mind. When natural knowledge was hardly existent, control of nature was impossible. Without power of control, there was no recourse save to build places of refuge in which man could live

in imagination, although not in fact. There is no
need to deny the grace and beauty of some of
these constructions. But when their imaginary
character is once made apparent, it is futile to
suppose that men can go on living and sustaining
life by them. When they are appealed to for support, the possibilities of the present are not per-
ceived, and its constructive potentialities remain
unutilized.

In reading many of the literary appreciations
of science, one would gather that until the rise of
modern science, men had not been aware that living in nature entails death and renders fortune
precarious and uncertain; "science" is even
treated as if it were responsible for the revelation
of the fact that nature is often a foe of human
interests and goods. But the very nature of the
creeds that men have entertained in the past and
of the rites they have practiced is proof that men
were overwhelmingly conscious of this fact. If
they had not been, they would not have resorted
to magic, miracles, myth and the consolations
and compensations of another world and life. As
long as these things were sincerely believed in,
dualism, anti-naturalism, had a meaning, for the

"other world" was then a reality. To surrender the belief and retain the dualism is temporarily possible for bewildered minds. It is a condition which it is impossible to maintain permanently. The alternative is to accept what science tells us of the world in which we live and to resolve to use the agencies it puts within our power to render nature more amenable to human desire and more contributory to human good. "Naturalism" is a word with all kinds of meanings. But a naturalism which perceives that man with his habits, institutions, desires, thoughts, aspirations, ideals and struggles, is within nature, an integral part of it, has the philosophical foundation and the practical inspiration for effort to employ nature as an ally of human ideals and goods such as no dualism can possibly provide.

There are those who welcome science provided it remain "pure"; they see that as a pursuit and contemplated object it is an addition to the enjoyed meaning of life. But they feel that its applications in mechanical inventions are the cause of many of the troubles of modern society. Undoubtedly these applications have brought new modes of unloveliness and suffering. I shall not attempt the impossible task of trying to strike a net balance of ills and enjoyments between the days before and after the practical use of science. The significant point is that application is still restricted. It touches our dealings with things but not with one another. We use scientific method in directing physical but not human energies. Consideration of the full application of science must accordingly be prophetic rather than a record of what has already taken place. Such prophecy is not however without foundation. Even as things are there is a movement in science which foreshadows, if its inherent promise be carried out, a more humane age. For it looks forward to a time when all individuals may share in the discoveries and thoughts of others, to the liberation and enrichment of their own experience.

No scientific inquirer can keep what he finds to himself or turn it to merely private account without losing his scientific standing. Everything discovered belongs to the community of workers. Every new idea and theory has to be submitted to this community for confirmation and test. There is an expanding community of coöperative effort and of truth. It is true enough that these traits are now limited to small groups having a somewhat technical activity. But the existence of such groups reveals a possibility of the present—one of the many possibilities that are a challenge to expansion, and not a ground for retreat and contraction.

Suppose that what now happens in limited circles were extended and generalized. Would the outcome be oppression or emancipation? Inquiry is a challenge, not a passive conformity; application is a means of growth, not of repression. The general adoption of the scientific attitude in human affairs would mean nothing less than a revolutionary change in morals, religion, politics and industry. The fact that we have limited its use so largely to technical matters is not a reproach to science, but to the human beings who use it for private ends and who strive to defeat its social application for fear of destructive effects upon their power and profit. A vision of a day in which the natural sciences and the technologies that flow from them are used as servants of a humane life constitutes the imagination that is relevant to our own time. A humanism that flees from science as an enemy denies the means by which a liberal humanism might become a reality.

The scientific attitude is experimental as well as intrinsically communicative. If it were generally applied, it would liberate us from the heavy burden imposed by dogmas and external standards. Experimental method is something other than the use of blow-pipes, retorts and reagents. It is the foe of every belief that permits habit and wont to dominate invention and discovery, and ready-made system to override verifiable fact. Constant revision is the work of experimental inquiry. By revision of knowledge and ideas, power to effect transformation is given us. This attitude, once incarnated in the individual mind, would find an operative outlet. If dogmas and institutions tremble when a new idea appears, this shiver is nothing to what would happen if the idea were armed with the means for the continuous discovery of new truth and the criticism of old belief. To "acquiesce" in science is dangerous only for those who would maintain affairs in the existing social order unchanged because of lazy habit or self-interest. For the scientific attitude demands faithfulness to whatever is discovered and steadfastness in adhering to new truth.

The "given" which science calls upon us to accept is not fixed; it is in process. A chemist does not study the elements in order to bow down before them; ability to produce transformations is the outcome. It is said, and truly, that we are now oppressed by the weight of science. But why? Some allowance has to be made, of course, for the time it takes to learn the uses of new means and to appropriate their potentialities. When these means are as radically new as is experimental science, the time required is correspondingly long. But aside from this fact, the multiplication of means and materials is an increase of opportunities and purposes. It marks a release of individuality for affections and deeds more congenial to its own nature. Even the derided bathtub has its individual uses; an individual is not perforce degraded because he has the chance to keep himself clean. The radio will make for standardization and regimentation only as long as individuals refuse to exercise the selective reaction that is theirs. The enemy is not material commodities, but the lack of the will to use them as instruments for achieving preferred possibilities. Imagine a society free from pecuniary domination, and it becomes self-evident that material commodities are invitations to individual taste and choice, and occasions for individual growth. If human beings are not strong and steadfast enough to accept the invitation and take advantage of the proffered occasion, let us put the blame where it belongs.

There is at least this much truth in economic determinism. Industry is not outside of human life, but within it. The genteel tradition shuts its eyes to this fact; emotionally and intellectually it pushes industry and its material phase out into a region remote from human values. To stop with mere emotional rejection and moral condemnation of industry and trade as materialistic is to leave them in this inhuman region where they operate as the instruments of those who employ them for private ends. Exclusion of this sort is an accomplice of the forces that keep things in the saddle. There is a subterranean partnership between those who employ the existing economic order for selfish pecuniary gain and those who turn their backs upon it in the interest of personal complacency, private dignity, and irresponsibility.

Every occupation leaves its impress on individual character and modifies the outlook on life of those who carry it on. No one questions this fact as respects wage-earners tied to the machine, or business men who devote themselves to pecuniary manipulations. Callings may have their roots in innate impulses of human nature but their pursuit does not merely "express" these impulses, leaving them unaltered; their pursuit determines intellectual horizons, precipitates knowledge and ideas, shapes desire and interest. This influence operates in the case of those who set up fine art, science, or religion as ends in themselves, isolated from radiation and expansion into other concerns (such radiation being what "application" signifies) as much as in the case of those who engage in industry. The alternatives are lack of application with consequent narrowing and overspecialization, and application with enlargement and increase of liberality. The narrowing in the case of industry pursued apart from social ends is evident to all thoughtful persons. Intellectual and literary folks who conceive themselves devoted to pursuit of pure truth and uncontaminated beauty too readily overlook the fact that a similar narrowing and hardening takes place in them. Their goods are more refined, but they are also engaged in acquisition; unless they are concerned with use, with expansive interactions, they too become monopolists of capital. And the monopolization of spiritual capital may in the end be more harmful than that of material capital.

The destructive effect of science upon beliefs long cherished and values once prized is, and quite naturally so, a great cause of dread of science and its applications in life. The law of inertia holds of the imagination and its loyalties as truly as of physical things. I do not suppose that it is possible to turn suddenly from these negative effects to possible positive and constructive ones. But as long as we refuse to make an effort to change the direction in which imagination looks at the world, as long as we remain unwilling to reëxamine old standards and values, science will continue to wear its negative aspect. Take science (including its application to the machine) for what it is, and we shall begin to

envisage it as a potential creator of new values
and ends. We shall have an intimation, on a wide
and generous scale, of the release, the increased
initiative, independence and inventiveness, which
science now brings in its own specialized fields to
the individual scientist. It will be seen as a means
of originality and individual variation. Even to
those sciences which delight in calling themselves
"pure," there is a significant lesson in the instinct
that leads us to speak of Newton's and Einstein's
law.

Because the free working of mind is one of
the greatest joys open to man, the scientific attitude, incorporated in individual mind, is something which adds enormously to one's enjoyment
of existence. The delights of thinking, of inquiry,
are not widely enjoyed at the present time. But
the few who experience them would hardly exchange them for other pleasures. Yet they are
now as restricted in quality as they are in the
number of those who share them. That is to say,
as long as "scientific" thinking confines itself to
technical fields, it lacks full scope and varied material. Its subject-matter is technical in the degree in which application in human life is shut

out. The mind that is hampered by fear lest
something old and precious be destroyed is the
mind that experiences fear of science. He who
has this fear cannot find reward and peace in the
discovery of new truths and the projection of
new ideals. He does not walk the earth freely,
because he is obsessed by the need of protecting
some private possession of belief and taste. For
the love of private possessions is not confined to
material goods.

It is a property of science to find its opportunities in problems, in questions. Since knowing
is inquiring, perplexities and difficulties are the
meat on which it thrives. The disparities and conflicts that give rise to problems are not something to be dreaded, something to be endured
with whatever hardihood one can command; they
are things to be grappled with. Each of us experiences these difficulties in the sphere of his
personal relations, whether in his more immediate contacts or in the wider associations conven-
tionally called "society." At present, personal
frictions are one of the chief causes of suffering.
I do not say all suffering would disappear with
the incorporation of scientific method into indi-

INDIVIDUALITY IN OUR DAY

vidual disposition; but I do say that it is now immensely increased by our disinclination to treat these frictions as problems to be dealt with intellectually. The distress that comes from being driven in upon ourselves would be largely relieved; it would in part be converted into the enjoyment that attends the free working of mind, if we took them as occasions for the exercise of thought, as problems having an objective direction and outlet.

We all experience, as I have said, the perplexities that arise in the intimacies of personal intercourse. The more remote relations of society also present their troubles. There is much talk of "social problems." But we rarely treat them as problems in the intellectual sense of that word. They are thought of as "evils" needing correction; as naughty or diabolic things to be "reformed." Our preoccupation with these ideas is proof of how far we are from taking the scientific attitude. I do not say that the attitude of the physician who regards his patient as a "beautiful case" is wholly ideal. But it is more wholesome and more promising than the persistence of the prescientific habit of anxious concerns with evils and their reform. The current way of treating criminality and criminals is, for example, reminiscent of the way in which diseases were once thought of and dealt with. Their origin was once believed to be moral and personal; some enemy, diabolic or human, was thought to have injected some alien substance or force into the person who was ailing. The possibility of effective treatment began when diseases were regarded as having an intrinsic origin in interactions of the organism and its natural environment. We are only just beginning to think of criminality as an equally intrinsic manifestation of interactions between an individual and the social environment. With respect to it, and with respect to so many other evils, we persist in thinking and acting in prescientific "moral" terms. This prescientific conception of "evil" is probably the greatest barrier that exists to that real reform which is identical with constructive remaking.

Because science starts with questions and inquiries it is fatal to all social system-making and programs of fixed ends. In spite of the bankruptcy of past systems of belief, it is hard to surrender our faith in system and in some wholesale belief. We continually reason as if the difficulty were in the particular system that has failed and as if we were on the point of now finally hitting upon one that is true as all the others were false. The real trouble is with the attitude of dependence upon any of them. Scientific method would teach us to break up, to inquire definitely and with particularity, to seek solutions in the terms of concrete problems as they arise. It is not easy to imagine the difference which would follow from the shift of thought to discrimination and analysis. Wholesale creeds and all - inclusive ideals are impotent in the face of actual situations; for doing always means the doing of something in particular. They are worse than impotent. They conduce to blind and vague emotional states in which credulity is at home, and where action, following the lead of overpowering emotion, is easily manipulated by the self-seekers who have kept their heads and wits. Nothing would conduce more, for example, to the elimination of war than the substitution of specific analysis of its causes for the wholesale love of "liberty, humanity, justice and civilization."

INDIVIDUALISM—OLD AND NEW

All of these considerations would lead to the conclusion that depression of the individual is the individual's own liability, were it not for the time it takes for a new principle to make its way deeply into individual mind on a large scale. But as time goes on, the responsibility becomes an individual one. For individuality is inexpugnable and it is of its nature to assert itself. The first move in recovery of an integrated individual is accordingly with the individual himself. In whatever occupation he finds himself and whatever interest concerns him, he is himself and no other, and he lives in situations that are in some respect flexible and plastic.

We are given to thinking of society in large and vague ways. We should forget "society" and think of law, industry, religion, medicine, politics, art, education, philosophy—and think of them in the plural. For points of contact are not the same for any two persons and hence the questions which the interests and occupations pose are never twice the same. There is no contact so immutable that it will not yield at some point. All these callings and concerns are the avenues through which the world acts upon us and we upon the world. There is no society at large, no business in general. Harmony with conditions is not a single and monotonous uniformity, but a diversified affair requiring individual attack.

Individuality is inexpugnable because it is a manner of distinctive sensitivity, selection, choice, response and utilization of conditions. For this reason, if for no other, it is impossible to develop integrated individuality by any all-embracing system or program. No individual can make the determination for anyone else; nor can he make it for himself all at once and forever. A native manner of selection gives direction and continuity, but definite expression is found in changing occasions and varied forms. The selective choice and use of conditions have to be continually made and remade. Since we live in a moving world and change with our interactions in it, every act produces a new perspective that demands a new exercise of preference. If, in the long run, an individual remains lost, it is because he has chosen irresponsibility; and if he remains wholly depressed, it is because he has chosen the course of easy parasitism.

Acquiescence, in the sense of drifting, is not

something to be achieved; it is something to be overcome, something that is "natural" in the sense of being easy. But it assumes a multitude of forms, and Rotarian applause for present conditions is only one of these forms. A different form of submission consists in abandoning the values of a new civilization for those of the past. To assume the uniform of some dead culture is only another means of regimentation. True integration is to be found in relevancy to the present, in active response to conditions as they present themselves, in the effort to make them over according to some consciously chosen possibility.

√ Individuality is at first spontaneous and unshaped; it is a potentiality, a capacity of development. Even so, it is a unique manner of acting in and with a world of objects and persons. It is not something complete in itself, like a closet in a house or a secret drawer in a desk, filled with treasures that are waiting to be bestowed on the world. Since individuality is a distinctive way of feeling the impacts of the world and of showing a preferential bias in response to these impacts, it develops into shape and form only through interaction with actual conditions; it is no more complete in itself than is a painter's tube of paint without relation to a canvas. The work of art is the truly individual thing; and it is the result of the interaction of paint and canvas through the medium of the artist's distinctive vision and power. In its determination, the potential individuality of the artist takes on visible and enduring form. The imposition of individuality as something made in advance always gives evidence of a mannerism, not of a manner. For the latter is something original and creative; something formed in the very process of creation of other things.

The future is always unpredictable. Ideals, including that of a new and effective individuality, must themselves be framed out of the possibilities of existing conditions, even if these be the conditions that constitute a corporate and industrial age. The ideals take shape and gain a content as they operate in remaking conditions. We may, in order to have continuity of direction, plan a program of action in anticipation of occasions as they emerge. But a program of ends and ideals if kept apart from sensitive and flexible method becomes an encumbrance. For its hard and rigid character assumes a fixed world and a static individual; and neither of these things exists. It implies that we can prophesy the future—an attempt which terminates, as someone has said, in prophesying the past or in its reduplication.

The same Emerson who said that "society is everywhere in conspiracy against its members" also said, and in the same essay, "accept the place the divine Providence has found for you, the society of your contemporaries, the connection of events." Now, when events are taken in disconnection and considered apart from the interactions due to the selecting individual, they conspire against individuality. So does society when it is accepted as something already fixed in institutions. But "the connection of events," and "the society of your contemporaries" as formed of moving and multiple associations, are the only means by which the possibilities of individuality can be realized.

Psychiatrists have shown how many disruptions and dissipations of the individual are due to his withdrawal from reality into a merely inner world. There are, however, many subtle forms of retreat, some of which are erected into systems of philosophy and are glorified in current literature. "It is in vain," said Emerson, "that we look for genius to reiterate its miracles in the old arts; it is its instinct to find beauty and holiness in new and necessary facts, in the field and roadside, in the shop and mill." To gain an integrated individuality, each of us needs to cultivate his own garden. But there is no fence about this garden: it is no sharply marked-off enclosure. Our garden is the world, in the angle at which it touches our own manner of being. By accepting the corporate and industrial world in which we live, and by thus fulfilling the precondition for interaction with it, we, who are also parts of the moving present, create ourselves as we create an unknown future.

CAPRICORN TITLES

138. *Walzel*, GERMAN ROMANTICISM. $1.45.
139. *Smith*, CONGRESSMAN FROM MISSISSIPPI. $1.95.
140. *Olcott*, MYTHS OF THE SUN. $1.75.
141. *Brown*, MIND YOUR LANGUAGE. $1.25.
142. *Wooldridge & East*, SPIRIT & PURPOSE OF GEOGRAPHY. $1.45.
143. *Seton-Watson*, NEW IMPERIALISM. $1.45.
144. *Maude*, SOUTH ASIA. $1.45.
145. *Cranston*, WESTERN POLITICAL PHILOSOPHERS. $1.45.
146. *Agar*, PERILS OF DEMOCRACY. $1.25.
147. *Walston*, AGRICULTURE UNDER COMMUNISM. $1.25.
148. *Daniel*, MYTH OR LEGEND. $1.25.
149. *DeVoto*, MARK TWAIN IN ERUPTION. $2.45.
150. *Prabhabanda*, THE WISDOM OF GOD. $2.45.
151. *Malla*, THE ANANGA RANGA. $.95.
152. *Kraft-Ebing*, PSYCHOPATHIA SEXUALIS. $.95.
153. *Bahm*, PHILOSOPHY OF THE BUDDHA. $1.45.
154. *Diderot*, DIALOGUES. $1.65.
155. *Hadas*, GIBBON'S THE DECLINE AND FALL OF THE ROMAN EMPIRE. $1.95.
156. *Veblen*, VEBLEN ON MARX, RACE, SCIENCE AND ECONOMICS. $2.95.
157. *Veblen*, THE VESTED INTERESTS AND THE COMMON MAN. $1.65.
158. *Cruikshank*, THE CRUIKSHANK FAIRY BOOK. $1.45.
159. *Lowry*, HEAR US O LORD FROM HEAVEN THY DWELLING PLACE. $1.85.
160. *Adler*, STUDIES IN ANALYTICAL PSYCHOLOGY. $1.95.
162. *Matthews*, FUGGER NEWSLETTERS. $1.95.
164. *Marx*, REVOLUTION AND COUNTER-REVOLUTION. $1.95.

CAPRICORN GIANTS

201. *Hauser*, DIET DOES IT. $1.95.
202. *Moscati*, ANCIENT SEMITIC CIVILIZATIONS. $2.65.
204. *Brockelman*, HISTORY OF ISLAMIC PEOPLES. $2.65.
205. *Salter*, CONDITIONED REFLEX THERAPY. $1.95.
207. *Davis*, CORPORATIONS. $2.45.
208. *Rodman*, CONVERSATIONS WITH ARTISTS. $1.65.
209. *Falls*, GREAT WAR. $2.15.
210. *Pius II*, MEMOIRS OF A RENAISSANCE POPE. $1.95.
213. *Cournos*, TREASURY OF CLASSIC RUSSIAN LITERATURE. $2.45.
215. *Guerdan*, BYZANTIUM. $1.65.
217. *Bradford*, OF PLYMOUTH PLANTATION. $1.95.
218. *Taylor*, COURSE OF GERMAN HISTORY. $1.65.
220. *Shelby Little*, GEORGE WASHINGTON. $1.95.
221. *Peterson*, ANCIENT MEXICO. $1.95.
224. *Krafft-Ebing*, ABERRATIONS OF SEXUAL LIFE. $1.95.
227. *Ernst-Loth*, REPORT ON THE AMERICAN COMMUNIST. $1.45.
228. *Adler*, THE PROBLEM CHILD. $1.95.
233. *Barraclough*, ORIGINS OF MODERN GERMANY. $2.45.
235. *Skeat*, ETYMOLOGICAL DICTIONARY. $3.45.
236. *Hauser*, GAYLORD HAUSER COOK BOOK. $1.65.
237. *Fulop Miller*, THE JESUITS. $2.45.
239. *Blitzer*, COMMONWEALTH OF ENGLAND. $1.65.

240. *Wright*, GREAT AMERICAN GENTLEMAN. $1.95.

246. *Weinberg*, THE MUCKRAKERS. $2.45.

247. *Hays*, FROM APE TO ANGEL. $3.45.

248. *James*, ANCIENT GODS. $2.25.

249. *Green*, LUTHER AND THE REFORMATION. $1.65.

250. *Filler*, THE ANXIOUS YEARS. $2.95.

251. *Ehrlich*, EHRLICH'S BLACKSTONE: RIGHTS OF PERSONS, RIGHTS OF THINGS. $2.95.

252. *Ehrlich*, EHRLICH'S BLACKSTONE: PRIVATE WRONGS, PUBLIC WRONGS. $2.95.

254. *Collis*, QUEST FOR SITA. $1.75.

255. *Nabokov*, INVITATION TO A BEHEADING. $1.65.

256. *Wedeck*, PUTNAM'S DARK & MIDDLE AGES READER. $1.95.

257. *Perroy*, THE HUNDRED YEARS WAR. $2.65.

258. *George*, LONDON LIFE IN 18TH CENTURY. $2.95.

259. *Rankin*, THE AMERICAN REVOLUTION. $1.95.

260. STALIN'S CORRESPONDENCE WITH ROOSEVELT & TRUMAN. $1.95.

261. STALIN'S CORRESPONDENCE WITH CHURCHILL & ATTLEE. $2.25.

262. *White*, A PURITAN IN BABYLON. $2.45.

263. *Czernin*, VERSAILLES 1919. $2.45.

264. *Filler*, PRESIDENT SPEAKS. $2.25.

265. *Ming*, HISTORY OF CHINESE LITERATURE. $2.65.

266. *Mead*, CHANGING CULTURE OF AN INDIAN TRIBE. $2.75.

268. *Churchill*, YEARS OF ADVENTURE. $2.25.

269. *Churchill*, YEARS OF GREATNESS. $1.95.

270. *Trefousse*, COLD WAR. $1.95.

271. *Louys*, SONGS OF BILITIS. $1.25.

272. *Sydenham*, FRENCH REVOLUTION. $2.25.

273. *Ley*, WILLY LEY'S EXOTIC ZOOLOGY. $2.65.

274. *Thomson*, CHAMBERLAIN LETTERS. $2.45.

275. *Orem*, MONTESSORI HANDBOOK. $1.65.

276. *Jenkins*, ELIZABETH THE GREAT. $1.95.

277. *Simpson*, GEOGRAPHY OF EVOLUTION. $1.75.

278. *Brown & Harris*, RESTORATION THEATRE. $1.65.

279. *Brown & Harris*, JACOBEAN THEATRE. $1.65.

280. *Kim*, PATTERNS OF COMPETITIVE COEXISTENCE. $2.95.

281. *Reader*, LIFE IN VICTORIAN ENGLAND. $1.95.

282. *Tomkeieff*, LIFE IN NORMAN ENGLAND. $1.95.

283. *Chamberlin*, EVERYDAY LIFE IN RENAISSANCE TIMES. $1.95.

284. *White*, EVERYDAY LIFE IN ANCIENT EGYPT. $1.75.

285. *Millis*, ARMS AND MEN. $2.45.

286. *Laven*, RENAISSANCE ITALY. $1.85.

287. *Wish*, DIARY OF SAMUEL SEWALL. $1.95.

288. *Verrill*, AMERICA'S ANCIENT CIVILIZATIONS. $1.95.

289. *Lander*, WARS OF THE ROSES. $1.95.

290. *Orem*, MONTESSORI FOR THE DISADVANTAGED. $1.65.

291. *Shukman*, LENIN & THE RUSSIAN REVOLUTION. $1.65.

292. *Cavendish*, THE BLACK ARTS. $1.95.

293. *Burland*, GODS OF MEXICO. $1.85.

294. *O'Connor*, SHORT HISTORY OF IRISH LITERATURE. $1.85.

295. *Clarens*, ILLUSTRATED HISTORY OF THE HORROR FILM. $2.75.

p 23
32